OECD ECONOMIC SURVEYS

1993-1994

AUSTRIA

ORGANISATION FOR ECONOMIC CO-OPERATION AND DEVELOPMENT

ORGANISATION FOR ECONOMIC CO-OPERATION AND DEVELOPMENT

Pursuant to Article 1 of the Convention signed in Paris on 14th December 1960, and which came into force on 30th September 1961, the Organisation for Economic Co-operation and Development (OECD) shall promote policies designed:

— to achieve the highest sustainable economic growth and employment and a rising standard of living in Member countries, while maintaining financial stability, and thus to contribute to the development of the world economy;

— to contribute to sound economic expansion in Member as well as non-member countries in the process of economic development; and

— to contribute to the expansion of world trade on a multilateral, non-discriminatory basis in accordance with international obligations.

The original Member countries of the OECD are Austria, Belgium, Canada, Denmark, France, Germany, Greece, Iceland, Ireland, Italy, Luxembourg, the Netherlands, Norway, Portugal, Spain, Sweden, Switzerland, Turkey, the United Kingdom and the United States. The following countries became Members subsequently through accession at the dates indicated hereafter: Japan (28th April 1964), Finland (28th January 1969), Australia (7th June 1971) and New Zealand (29th May 1973). The Commission of the European Communities takes part in the work of the OECD (Article 13 of the OECD Convention).

3 2280 00497 9878

Publié également en français.

Table of contents

Tables

Diagrams

BASIC STATISTICS OF AUSTRIA

THE LAND

Area (1 000 sq. km)	84	Major cities, 1991 census (thousands of	
Agricultural area (1 000 sq. km) 1990	35	inhabitants):	
Exploited forest area (1 000 sq. km)	32	Vienna	1 553
		Graz	232
		Linz	203
		Salzburg	144
		Innsbruck	115

THE PEOPLE

Population 1.1.92, thousands	7 884	Net migration, 1992, thousands	46.8
Number of inhabitants per sq. km	94	Total employment,[1] monthly average	
Net natural increase, 1992	12 140	1992, thousands	2 997
Net natural increase		*of which:*	
per 1 000 inhabitants, 1992	1.5	in industry[2]	521

PRODUCTION

Gross domestic product in 1992		Industrial origin of GDP at market	
(Sch billion)	2 029	prices, 1992 (per cent):	
GDP per head, US$	23 419	Agriculture	2.4
Gross fixed capital formation in 1992		Industry	26.0
Per cent of GDP	25	Construction	7.6
Per head, US$	5 777	Other	64.0

THE GOVERNMENT

Per cent of GDP in 1992:		Composition of Federal Parliament	
Public consumption	18.3	(number of seats):	
General government current revenue	48.7	Socialist party	79
Federal Government debt, end 1991	46.2	Austrian People's party	60
		Liberal party	28
		Greens	10
		Liberal Forum	5
		Independent	1
		Last general election: October 1990	

FOREIGN TRADE

Exports of goods and services,		Imports of goods and services,	
as per cent of GDP, 1992	39.7	as per cent of GDP, 1992	38.4
Main exports in 1992 (per cent		Main imports in 1992 (per cent	
of total merchandise exports):		of total merchandise imports):	
Food, beverages, tobacco	3.3	Food, beverages, tobacco	4.9
Raw materials and energy	5.1	Raw materials and energy	9.3
Machinery and transport equipment	38.9	Machinery and transport equipment	39.5
Chemicals	8.6	Chemicals	9.8
Other finished and semi-manufactured		Other finished and semi-manufactured	
products	44.1	products	36.5

THE CURRENCY

Monetary unit: Schilling		Currency units per US$,	
		average of daily figures:	
		Year 1993	11.63
		February 1994	12.22

1. Wage and salary earners.
2. Including administrative personnel.
Note: An international comparison of certain basic statistics is given in an annex table.

This Survey is based on the Secretariat's study prepared for the annual review of Austria by the Economic and Development Review Committee on 24th February 1994.

•

After revisions in the light of discussions during the review, final approval of the Survey for publication was given by the Committee on 31st March 1994.

•

The previous Survey of Austria was issued in April 1993.

Introduction

The recent cyclical downturn has served to demonstrate the resilience of the Austrian economy. Despite severe external stresses, stemming from the European recession, exchange rate appreciation and the structural challenge of opening the economy to the east, the 1993 decline in GDP was relatively mild. Consumer sentiment has remained surprisingly buoyant, despite heightened job insecurity, and this has been a major stabilising force in the economy. Moreover, the benefits of social consensus have once again been demonstrated in recent moderate industrial wage agreements, which are helping to stabilise unemployment and cushion the loss in competitiveness. At the same time, international investors' confidence in Austria's anti-inflationary monetary and exchange rate policies has permitted short-term rates to fall below German ones, while the government has exploited the available scope for fiscal manœuvre by allowing automatic stabilisers to operate and even to provide a small discretionary boost to investment.

Weaker activity has, however, also revealed certain underlying problems. Inflation has responded only slowly to economic slack, due to stubborn inflation in the sheltered sectors and to the fact that terms-of-trade gains have not been fully passed on to consumers. Unemployment, though low, has been secularly increasing and is becoming associated with a highly skewed employment distribution which discriminates against older and longer-term unemployed, suggesting an insufficient capacity to reabsorb and retrain certain categories of workers in the context of the rapid structural changes that are occurring. And the prospects for fiscal consolidation have deteriorated significantly, due, in part, to the recession and to the net budgetary burden of taxation and social spending initiatives. These three elements constitute potential sources of medium-term tension to set against the prospects for a gradual upturn in activity and the prospective longer-term benefits of EU membership.

Following a discussion of the sources of the recession, Part I discusses the problems of rising unemployment and inflation inertia, and the implications of the latter for external competitiveness and the trade balance. Part II covers recent macroeconomic policy developments and examines short-term economic prospects in light of these policies. Part III focuses on public sector issues, particularly the institutional background to public expenditure control relating to "fiscal federalism" and the management of the large number of fiscal and para-fiscal bodies through which budgetary policy is exercised in Austria. Part IV presents the Conclusions.

I. Recent Developments

Overview

Although moderate in comparison with the downturn in Austria's major trading partners, the current recession has been somewhat worse than those experienced in 1975 and 1981 (Diagram 1). The downturn which began around the middle of 1992 intensified sharply at the turn of the year, resulting in a real GDP decline of 1 per cent for the first half of 1993 (from a year earlier). However, the rate of decline slowed markedly from the first to second quarters, and the economy appears to have stabilised some time in the autumn months, as the year-long decline in industrial production started to abate and construction activity and domestic and foreign orders started to pick up (Diagram 2, panels A and B). In spite of still-depressed business confidence and continuing export weakness, these factors suggest a return to positive growth in the fourth quarter, implying a full-year GDP decline of perhaps 1/2 per cent (Table 1).

Though the 1993 growth outcome was only slightly weaker than projected in the previous *Survey*, its demand composition was markedly different: investment and exports turned out to be much weaker than expected, but this was compensated by stronger private and public consumption.[1] This pattern of demand resulted in the recession being felt almost exclusively in the open industrial sector (Table 2). The decline in aggregate output and the rise in unemployment were both tempered by continued positive – though weakening – growth and net job creation in the domestically-oriented sectors. Nevertheless, the standardised rate of unemployment increased from 3 1/2 to 4 1/4 per cent between 1992 and 1993, while labour productivity declined. As a result, unit labour costs rose and, despite the economic slack, the rate of increase in the consumer price index slowed down only modestly, from 4 per cent in 1992 to 3 3/4 per cent in 1993. This further exacerbated the competitiveness loss stemming

11

Diagram 1. MACROECONOMIC PERFORMANCE

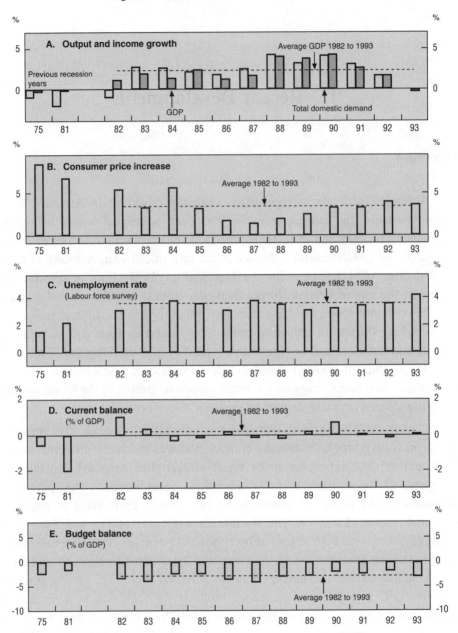

Source: OECD.

Diagram 2. **THE BUSINESS CYCLE**

Percentage change from year ago, 3-month moving average

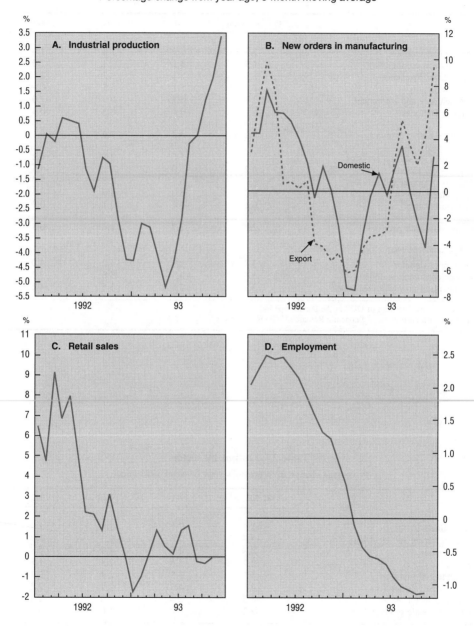

A. Industrial production

B. New orders in manufacturing

Domestic

Export

1992   93

C. Retail sales

D. Employment

1992   93

Source: Austrian Institute for Economic Research (WIFO) and OECD, *Main Economic indicators.*

Table 1. Demand and output

Percentage change from previous year, constant 1983 prices

	1981-90 average	1991	1992	1993
Private consumption	2.5	2.9	1.8	1.0
Government consumption	1.3	3.1	2.4	2.0
Gross fixed investment	2.2	5.1	2.7	-2.6
Construction	1.8	5.1	5.5	0.8
Machinery and equipment	2.7	4.7	-0.9	-7.0
Change in stocks [1]	-0.1	-0.4	-0.3	-0.3
Total domestic demand	**2.1**	**3.3**	**2.0**	**-0.1**
Exports of goods and services	5.1	5.6	2.8	0.2
of which: Goods	6.2	3.0	2.1	-4.5
Imports of goods and services	4.7	6.3	2.8	1.0
of which: Goods	4.9	6.0	1.3	-4.3
Foreign balance [1]	0.1	-0.4	-0.1	-0.4
Gross domestic product	**2.2**	**2.7**	**1.6**	**-0.5**
Memorandum items:				
GDP price deflator	3.8	3.9	4.2	4.0
Private consumption deflator	3.6	3.5	3.8	3.6
Standardised unemployment rate	3.3	3.5	3.6	4.2

1. Change as a per cent of GDP in the previous period.
Source: Austrian Institute of Economic Research (WIFO).

Table 2. Output by sector

Percentage change from previous year, constant 1983 prices

	1981-90 average	1991	1992	1993
Agriculture	1.5	-7.1	-3.4	1.9
Manufacturing and electricity	2.3	2.6	0.3	-2.7
Construction	0.3	4.5	4.9	0.8
Services	2.7	3.6	2.3	1.1
Trade and transport	3.1	3.8	2.4	-0.4
Other private services	3.1	4.0	2.2	2.2
Public sector	1.5	2.4	2.0	2.3
Gross domestic product	2.2	2.7	1.6	-0.5

Source: WIFO.

from exchange rate appreciation, but despite this, the current account remained close to balance.

Nature of the recession

Contraction in exports and investment

Sharply declining exports of goods – reflecting both the foreign recession and an effective appreciation of the schilling – can be seen as the chief proximate cause of the recession. These have resulted in falling sales and profits in industry, leading in turn to rapid reductions in capacity utilisation, depressed business confidence, record bankruptcies and job losses[2] (Diagram 3, panel D). Goods export volumes, whose growth had already slowed notably in 1992, are estimated to have fallen by 6 per cent in 1993. This induced a decline in machinery and equipment investment of 3 per cent in 1992 and a further 8 per cent in 1993. Indeed, the fact that a large part of Austrian manufacturing firms are major suppliers to western German firms means that any cyclical downturn in western Germany (such as occurred in 1993) is keenly felt, especially in the auto sector. The sharp depreciations of the currencies of major competitor countries such as Italy, the United Kingdom, and Scandinavian countries further dampened short term export prospects and business confidence, as did the slowing of imports of the eastern countries.

Apart from export weakness, another factor which may have reduced the expected rate of return to investment was the still high level of real interest rates. Although nominal long-term interest rates had already begun to decline in 1991, nearing their historical lows of around 6 per cent by end-1993, real rates have remained high at least as measured by producer prices, as the rate of inflation of the wholesale price index was slightly negative in both 1992 and 1993. The inverted yield curve could also have discouraged real investments, as a relatively high short term interest rate tended to favour investments in risk-free financial instruments. Indeed, much as in Germany, a recovery of investment has histori-cally always been preceded by a normalisation of the yield curve. However, credit subsidies, though declining in recent years in the area of non-residential investment (see next chapter),[3] may have acted to dampen the impact of high interest rates on investment.

Diagram 3. COMPOSITION OF DEMAND[1]
Percentage changes from previous period

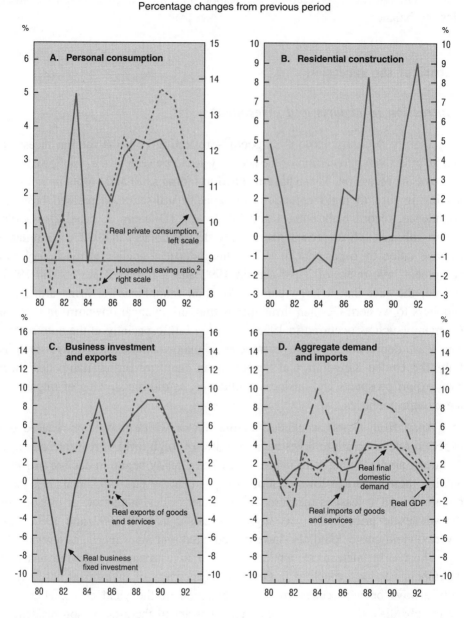

1. 1993 estimated.
2. As a percentage of disposable income.
Source: OECD.

The February 1993 "stabilisation package" attempted to offset some of the underlying weakness in private investment, the chief instrument in this regard being a temporary increase in the investment tax allowance (from 20 to 30 per cent, for fourteen months). This was intended to encourage a bringing forward of investments into 1993, against the background of persistent weakness in business confidence.

On the other hand, the negative contribution to GDP growth of falling merchandise exports and business investment was partly offset by large declines in merchandise import volumes, as demand components with a high-import content – durables consumption, machinery and equipment investment, and exports of goods – all contracted quite sharply (Diagram 3, panels C and D). Also, net services exports did not react as strongly to world recession and declining competitiveness as did goods, although tourism exports fell by about 2 per cent in volume terms.

Sustained housing and consumption demand

Construction investment, in particular residential construction, also continued to provide a positive stimulus to output, despite slowing down markedly (Diagram 3, panel B). Though some of this deceleration was the result of unusually bad weather in the early months of the year, it also reflected an increasing saturation of demand for residential structures and office buildings. However, in the latter months of the year, construction activity appears to have been regaining in strength. It also benefited from a continuing high rate of government investment, including the accelerated implementation of projects planned for 1994. Interest rates are thought to have only a small impact on construction demand due to the large subsidy component in housing and building loan costs.

Private consumption has exhibited surprising strength in the face of recession. Real disposable incomes stagnated in both 1992 and 1993 due to rising unemployment and slowing real wage growth. A large decline in the savings ratio in both years enabled consumption growth to remain comfortably positive (Diagram 3, panel A). This followed sharp increases in the savings ratio during the boom years 1990-91, to near-historic highs of around $13\frac{1}{2}$ per cent. Though household confidence in Austria is traditionally resilient to cyclical swings,[4] an added confidence-boosting factor in this recession may have been the anticipation of major tax cuts in 1994. Also, the reform to the system of family allowances, instituted in early 1993, favoured large families and could have boosted consumption propensities through such redistributional channels (see next chapter).

Declining real short-term interest rates may further have favoured consumption by reducing the remuneration from savings. However, the interest rate responsiveness of consumption is on the whole weak, due to the prevalence of small-type savings accounts paying less than market rates of interest and the relatively scant recourse to consumer credit.[5] A relatively more important stimulus to consumption may have come from the 1993 increase in the tax on interest income, from 10 to 22 per cent. Nevertheless, the composition of household expenditures reveals an adjustment of spending patterns, as major purchases for durable goods (mainly autos) were cut back significantly while growth of non-durables consumption held steady.

Public consumption sustained a rate of growth of about 2 per cent in both 1992 and 1993, also helping to support output growth. Zero growth of real public consumption had originally been planned for 1993, as part of the planned budget consolidation programme. However, the recession caused the government to defer its budget consolidation plans.

Labour market trends

Declining productivity

The recession has resulted in declining productivity of both labour and capital (Diagram 4). In past recessions, capital productivity tended to rise (as elsewhere), with a slowing in the growth in the capital stock. This contrasts with the experience in the present recession, which has continued the recent trend for the capital/output ratio to rise and capital productivity to fall. At the same time, labour productivity declined in 1992, and remained flat in 1993. This may reflect a certain amount of labour hoarding, which is typical of economic downturns in Austria and can be regarded as stabilising so long as wage costs remain under control. It has, however, led to a falling capital income share, reversing the trend of the 1980s (Diagram 4, panel C). Moreover, weakening labour productivity growth even prior to the recession may also have reflected developments in labour supply: a strong increase in the supply of foreign labour starting in

18

Diagram 4. **PRODUCTIVITY OF LABOUR AND CAPITAL**

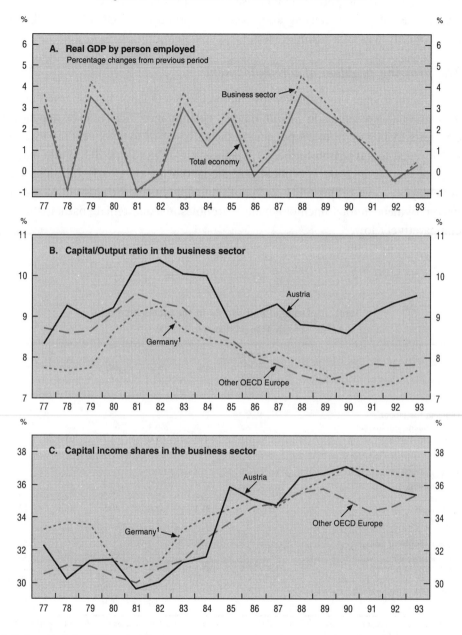

1. Up to and including 1990 western Germany.
Source: WIFO and OECD, *Economic Outlook* No. 54, December 1993.

1989 caused a disproportionate increase of new jobs in the lower-skilled and less productive categories, causing a slowdown of productivity growth even though the economy was in a boom.

The growing problem of unemployment

Unemployment remains low by international standards, but the trend points to a gradual worsening in labour market performance. The rate of dependent unemployment rose from 2½ per cent in the early-1980s to 6 per cent in 1992 and is estimated to have risen further to 7 per cent in 1993 (Table 3).[6] While part of the more recent increase is cyclical, and the labour market clearly functions well with respect to wage flexibility and youth unemployment, the share of long-term unemployment in total unemployment is troublesome and female participation is comparatively low.

Table 3. **Demand and supply in the labour market**

Change from previous year in '000

	Average annual change 1985-89	1989	1990	1991	1992	1993
Demand for labour						
Dependent employment[1]	16.5	51.8	66.4	68.7	58.5	-2.3
Self-employment	-7.1	-6.5	-5.0	-2.7	-5.4	-7.5
Total	9.4	45.3	61.4	66.0	53.1	-9.8
Supply of labour						
Foreigners	..	17.1	51.2	47.7	18.7	6.5
Migration	..	-5.0	-5.2	-3.0	2.3	2.5
Domestic	..	23.8	32.0	40.5	40.1	13.5
Total	16.4	35.8	78.0	85.2	61.1	22.5
Excess supply of labour						
Unemployment	7.0	-9.5	16.6	19.2	8.1	32.3
Unemployment level	153.6	149.2	165.8	185.0	193.1	225.4
Registered unemployment rate[2]	5.2	5.0	5.4	5.8	5.9	6.9
of which: Unemployed for over one year[2]	..	0.7	0.7	0.9	1.0	..

1. Including dependent employees on maternity leave: +9 900 in 1991, +34 800 in 1992, and +7 600 (estimated) in 1993.
2. Per cent of total dependent labour force.
Source: WIFO and Österreichisches Statistisches Zentralamt, Statistische Nachrichten.

From 1960 to 1980, both supply and demand factors favoured the maintenance of virtually full employment.[7] Labour supply growth was restricted by slow population growth, longer schooling periods and earlier retirements, a rapid build-up of family benefits which slowed the rise in female participation rates, and shorter working hours and longer holidays.[8] The demand for labour was kept high partly through expansionary public spending policies.[9] While such policies kept visible unemployment low, this entailed high costs in the form of a continuous growth of subsidies to the nationalised industries. Under the depressive impact of the second oil shock, rising budget deficits narrowed the scope for fiscal support to demand, and the nationalised industries could no longer act as a shock-absorber for the labour market. Thus, unemployment tended to rise in the 1980s. Moreover, strong output and employment growth from 1987 to 1991 failed to alleviate unemployment as there was also a surge in labour supply due to greatly increased immigration mainly from former Yugoslavia and other economies in transition in central and eastern Europe.

The cyclical downturn that began in 1992 has caused a renewed increase in unemployment. In 1992, unemployment grew only slightly from the previous year. However, correcting for a large increase in the number of women on maternity leave due to greatly expanded benefits[10] – who are officially counted as still employed – the rate of growth of employment was only $\frac{1}{2}$ per cent. Jobs were lost in manufacturing, especially in metalworking, textiles and clothing, but employment continued to expand in private services and in the public sector. In 1993, job losses in the open sectors intensified due to deepening foreign recession and increased competition from both eastern Europe and the devaluing countries of OECD Europe. However, a continuing growth of jobs in the service sectors, in particular in the public sector, limited the overall fall in employment to less than $\frac{1}{2}$ per cent. Unemployment growth was also limited by a sharp decline in labour force growth reflecting reduced immigration, as the quota of work permits for foreign workers was lowered from 10 to 9 per cent of the labour force.[11] Even so, the rate of unemployment rose by 1 per centage point.

The secular rise in the level of unemployment has been associated with a trend toward long duration unemployment, and – linked with this development – unemployment among older workers. Largely due to the apprenticeship system, youth unemployment is not a major problem as elsewhere in the OECD. But unemployment among workers over 50 years of age is high and has been rising

Diagram 5. UNEMPLOYMENT STRUCTURE
1992

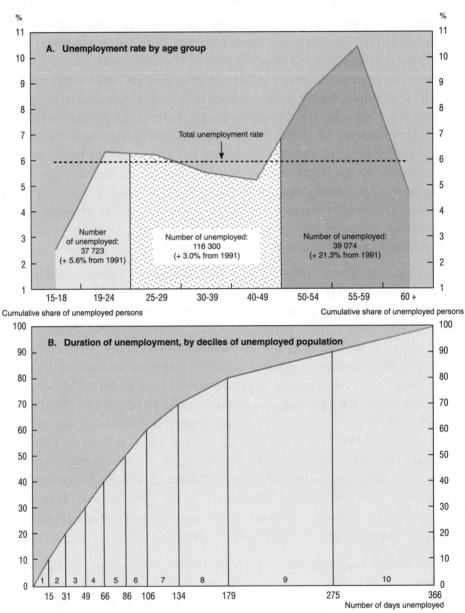

A. Unemployment rate by age group

Total unemployment rate ↓

Number of unemployed: 37 723 (+ 5.6% from 1991)

Number of unemployed: 116 300 (+ 3.0% from 1991)

Number of unemployed: 39 074 (+ 21.3% from 1991)

15-18   19-24   25-29   30-39   40-49   50-54   55-59   60 +

Cumulative share of unemployed persons

Cumulative share of unemployed persons

B. Duration of unemployment, by deciles of unemployed population

1   2   3   4   5   6   7   8   9   10

15   31   49   66   86   106   134   179   275   366

Number of days unemployed

Source: Austrian Central Statistical Office, Statistische Nachrichten, Nov. 1993.

much more rapidly than for other age groups (Diagram 5). This has occurred despite the marked reduction of the effective pensionable age during the 1980s – which has significantly reduced labour supply and kept down measured unemployment. The data also reveal the enormous polarisation implied by growing longer-term unemployment: the upper two deciles of the total number of unemployed workers bore half of the unemployment burden (workdays lost) in 1992; while the lower two deciles, only one-twelfth. Women, workers over 50, and service-sector workers stand disproportionately high risks of remaining unemployed.[12]

Inflation inertia in the sheltered sector

Austria's centralised system of wage bargaining tends to make for a relatively high degree of real wage flexibility. However, in periods of cyclical downturn, the adoption of too favourable economic assumptions may deliver wage awards which are economically justified only in the high-productivity sectors. Hence, rapid wage growth over the past few years has resulted in strongly rising labour costs given weak, even negative, productivity growth in the non-industrial sectors (Table 4). Mainly in response to such continuing high unit labour cost growth, Austria's relative inflation performance worsened markedly between 1990 and 1993[13] (Diagram 6). Growing industrial unemployment has more recently begun to have a moderating impact: the autumn-1993 agreements in important industrial sectors point to a slowing in the aggregate effective wage from 4³/₄ per cent in 1993 to 2³/₄ per cent in 1994, roughly equal to the expected rate of inflation in that year (see next chapter). Thus unit labour costs, and hence inflation, are expected to respond to the growing economic slack during 1994.

Owing to exchange rate appreciation, significant terms-of-trade gains occurred in both 1992 and 1993 (see below), implying a potential downward pull on inflation. However, these appear to have been used to boost traders' profit margins rather than to reduce final-goods prices – profit margins continued to widen despite a collapse of profits in many areas of industry. As a result, the consumer price increase for industrial goods has remained at 3 per cent per year since 1990 (Diagram 7). Equally persistent and yet higher rates of inflation are to be found in the rental, housing, and other service sectors, where high labour costs have been fully reflected in prices due to the labour-intensive and sheltered nature

Table 4. **Wages and productivity**

Percentage change from previous year

	1990	1991	1992	1993
Whole economy				
Wages[1]	5.2	6.5	5.6	4.8
Output	4.2	2.7	1.7	−0.5
Employment	2.3	2.4	2.0	−0.0
Productivity	1.9	0.4	−0.3	−0.4
Industry[2]				
Wages[1]	7.5	5.7	6.0	5.5
Production	7.7	2.2	−0.7	−3.5
Employment	1.6	−1.1	−3.4	−6.5
Productivity	6.0	3.3	2.8	3.2
Non-industry				
Wages[1]	4.6	6.9	5.7	4.9
Output	4.2	2.8	2.1	0.4
Employment	2.5	3.1	3.1	1.3
Productivity	1.6	−0.3	−1.0	−0.9

1. Average monthly wages and salaries per employed worker.
2. Excluding energy, construction and crafts.
Source: WIFO and OECD estimates.

Diagram 6. **INFLATION AND ITS SOURCES**[1]

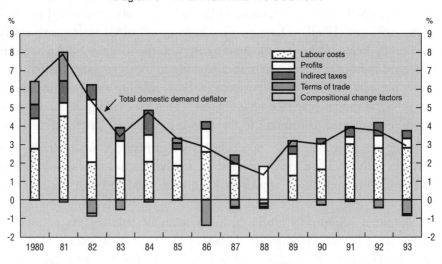

1. See Technical Annex for the decomposition of the total domestic deflator.
Source: OECD, *National Accounts.*

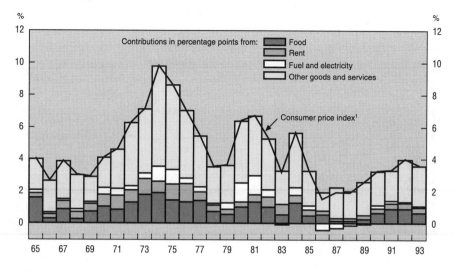

Diagram 7. **CONTRIBUTIONS TO CONSUMER PRICE INFLATION**

1. Annual percentage change.
Source: OECD, *Main Economic Indicators.*

of these sectors. Public charges and indirect taxes have also been raised.[14] Food and energy prices have remained as the only areas where consumers have gained from lower (world) prices.

International competitiveness and the current account

The current account has been in approximate balance for most of the past ten years, with the large trade deficit being offset by a services surplus, dominated by tourism exports (Diagram 8). In 1993, this continued to be the case, despite Austria's relatively strong cyclical position and large competitiveness losses over the 1992-93 period (Diagram 9).

One major reason for the relatively favourable 1993 result was that the current account benefited significantly from the "J-curve" effects of schilling appreciation. Table 5 provides an approximate method of calculating the impact of the exchange rate appreciation on trade prices (defined as the trade deflators

25

Diagram 8. **CURRENT ACCOUNT DEVELOPMENTS**
As per cent of GDP

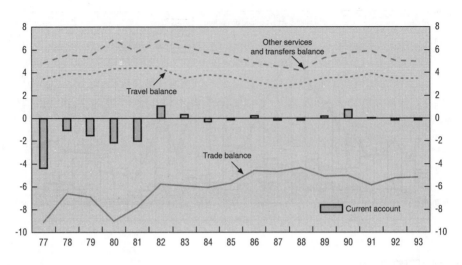

Source: WIFO.

for total goods and services). The cumulative 1992-93 change in import prices was –2.1 per cent – ostensibly a pass-through of slightly less than one-half of the concurrent exchange rate change of 4.7 per cent. However, since foreign suppliers' export prices were increased at the same time by almost 2½ per cent in local currency terms, in reality over 90 per cent of the schilling appreciation appears to have been reflected in import prices.[15]

In fact, however, as noted above, virtually all of these terms of trade gains were retained by Austrian importers, rather than being further passed through to retail prices, *i.e.* to the final consumers of imports. This, in turn, would help to explain the surprising weakness of import volumes in the face of sharply declining import prices relative to domestic prices (Table 6). Indeed, an analysis of the contributions to changes in manufactures import volumes shows that, while perhaps two-thirds of the volume decline can be attributed to cyclical domestic demand factors, falling import prices should have had an offsetting positive impact on import demand. Import volumes were also exceptionally depressed by

Diagram 9. **MEASURES OF COMPETITIVENESS**[1]

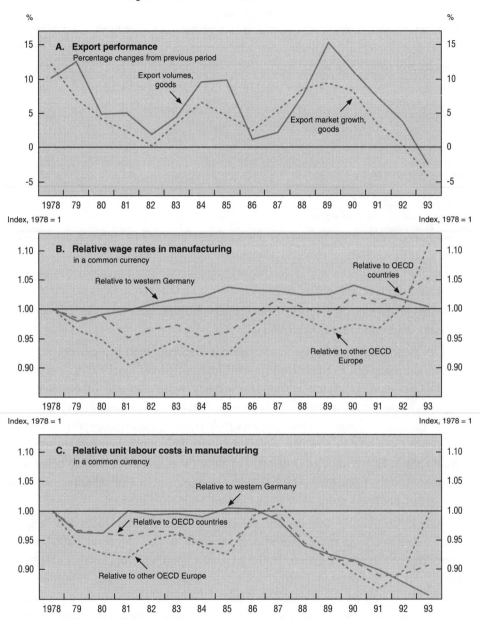

A. Export performance
Percentage changes from previous period

Export volumes, goods

Export market growth, goods

Index, 1978 = 1

B. Relative wage rates in manufacturing
in a common currency

Relative to OECD countries

Relative to western Germany

Relative to other OECD Europe

Index, 1978 = 1

C. Relative unit labour costs in manufacturing
in a common currency

Relative to western Germany

Relative to OECD countries

Relative to other OECD Europe

Index, 1978 = 1

1. Relative to trade weighted average of trading partners.
Source: OECD.

Table 5. **Exchange rate pass-through, 1992-93**

Per cent changes

	1992	1993	Cumulative
Nominal effective exchange rate (a)	1.9	2.7	4.7
Foreign competitors' export price[1] (b)	–0.8	3.2	2.4
Import price[2] (c)	–0.8	–1.3	–2.1
Exchange rate effect (c – b)	0.0	–4.4	–4.4
Rate of pass-through, cumulative $\frac{(c-b)}{a}$			93.5
Memorandum items:			
Export price[2] (d)	1.0	0.6	1.6
Relative export price (d + a – b)	3.7	0.1	3.9

1. In foreign currency terms; proxied by export prices in manufacturing and services, representing 90% of total exports of goods and services.
2. Trade deflators for total goods and services.
Source: OECD calculations.

a number of quotas on imports from eastern Europe, in particular on cement, fertilisers, and agricultural machinery.[16]

Developments in Austrian export prices also benefited the current account (at least temporarily), as these rose in schilling terms over the 1992-93 period by over 1½ per cent, implying a foreign currency price increase of 6½ per cent – 4 per centage points more than competitors' export prices and nearly equal to the full exchange rate rise. This suggests that, overall, Austrian exporters sought to stabilise their schilling prices, rather than cut their profit margins to preserve market shares. However, closer inspection shows that this price-setting behaviour emanates entirely from the service sectors, as export prices of manufactures and other goods declined more or less in tandem with world prices.

Largely reflecting the greater severity of the foreign recession, export volumes declined even more than import volumes, so that the contribution of net exports to growth was negative. In the case of export volumes of manufactures, virtually all of the volume decline can be attributed to declining export market growth, dominated by the German recession (Table 6). Hence there was no loss of market share in 1993. However, the large real effective exchange rate appreciation (7½ per cent during 1992-93), reflecting rising unit labour costs relative to those in competitor countries, points to extensive profit pressures in exporting

Table 6. Determinants of trade volumes

Per cent change from previous year

	1989	1990	1991	1992	1993
Export volumes[1]	15.8	10.5	8.3	3.9	–4.4
Determined by					
Export market growth[1]	9.5	8.0	3.0	0.3	–4.5
Export relative price[1]	–9.7	4.5	–6.0	1.0	–0.4
Export deflator[1]	–3.5	–0.9	–4.2	–1.8	–0.1
Competitor's export price[1,2]	6.6	–4.8	1.4	–3.0	0.2
Indirectly determined by					
Relative unit labour cost (real effective exchange rate)	–4.7	1.4	–1.1	3.3	4.1
Domestic unit labour cost[1]	–0.5	1.0	2.5	3.0	2.5
Foreign unit labour cost[1,2]	4.2	–0.4	3.6	–0.3	–1.6
Import volumes[1]	11.7	12.2	2.8	3.6	–1.3
Determined by					
Domestic demand (import-weighted)	5.6	6.1	3.9	2.1	0.1
Import relative price	–0.9	–5.2	0.6	–5.3	–6.0
Import deflator[1]	2.3	–3.1	4.2	–1.8	–3.3
Domestic demand deflator	3.1	2.6	3.4	3.7	2.9

1. In manufacturing.
2. In schilling terms.
Source: OECD estimates.

industry which have probably acted to restrain incentives to export in the near-term (see next chapter).

The geographical composition of goods exports has been affected by relative demand and price changes (Table 7). Exports to Germany declined sharply due both to recession there and reduced competitiveness *vis-à-vis* third countries. Exports to the depreciating countries in Europe fell even more precipitously. The growth rate of exports to eastern Europe, although slowing, held up relatively well in view of the ongoing declines in Austrian competitiveness. Exports to east Asia and the United States, by contrast, increased strongly due to these economies' greater dynamism as well as to a decline of the schilling against the dollar.

Tourism volumes clearly reflected the foreign recession and adverse relative price developments in the service sectors. Summer tourism, which is highly cyclically and price sensitive, fell off substantially, with foreign overnight stays

Table 7. **Geographical composition of exports and imports**

Percentage changes

	1989 level (Sch billion)	1990	1991	1992	1993
Exports to					
Germany	153.9	13.8	7.0	3.7	−6.5
Devaluing countries of Europe [1]	92.9	0.5	−2.0	−0.9	−14.2
Eastern Europe	39.6	17.2	7.9	7.4	4.8
Hungary	8.7	21.8	37.3	7.2	6.3
Czech Republic and Slovakia	5.0	74.6	4.9	51.3	11.0
Poland	5.2	−15.0	68.4	−5.5	−9.0
Former Yugoslavia [2]	9.2	35.9	−23.3	−3.0	11.5
Former USSR	11.5	−11.8	−8.0	−14.3	−4.6
United States	15.0	0.1	−9.4	−5.1	24.2
Dynamic Asian economies	5.7	−0.2	4.2	10.3	17.5
All other	122.2	8.0	−0.5	−1.2	−1.6
Total	429.3	8.9	2.6	1.7	−4.2
Imports from					
Germany	226.8	8.3	3.9	0.1	−8.0
Devaluating countries of Europe [1]	83.9	9.1	5.8	0.8	−3.1
Eastern Europe	33.4	10.6	8.5	4.2	−2.1
Hungary	7.8	12.4	30.2	4.6	−9.8
Czech Republic and Slovakia	6.7	−4.5	15.7	49.8	10.1
Poland	4.4	15.8	11.8	−10.7	−7.3
Former Yugoslavia [3]	6.0	7.1	−8.8	−12.4	−4.2
Former USSR	8.5	20.9	−5.3	−12.3	−2.8
United States	18.6	8.4	15.9	0.3	6.3
Dynamic Asian economies	12.2	2.2	20.2	−6.1	−3.6
All other	139.8	8.4	7.4	0.1	−3.7
Total	514.7	8.4	6.2	0.3	−4.9

1. Italy, Spain, Portugal, Greece, United Kingdom, Norway, Sweden and Finland.
2. Of which respectively in 1992 and 1993, Sch 1 916 million and Sch 2 824 million to Croatia; Sch 5 642 million and Sch 6 794 million to Slovenia.
3. Of which in 1993, Sch 1 377 million from Croatia and Sch 3 376 million from Slovenia.
Source: Austrian National Bank and OECD, *Monthly statistics of foreign trade.*

falling 6 per cent below year-earlier levels during the May-to-October period.[17] Partly compensating, however, was an exceptionally good winter tourist season owing to very good skiing conditions in the early months of 1993. The 1993 declines in goods and tourism export volumes were also to some extent offset by buoyant growth in items such as transmission of information, technical, scientific and economic consulting. A large part of such receipts are associated with the growing integration with eastern Europe, for which such services are in high demand and which Austria is well-placed to provide. Growth of this category was also high on the import side, as Austria was a recipient of such products from other western countries.

II. Macroeconomic policies and the short-term outlook

Overview

Both unemployment and output fluctuations have tended to be smaller in Austria than in OECD Europe generally, while inflation has been lower and current account disturbances less marked (Diagram 10). This relatively balanced economic performance owes much to a monetary regime which has relied on exchange-rate stability – expressed since 1981 in terms of a fixed parity with the Deutschemark – as the anchor for wage and price expectations. Further macroeconomic ingredients have been a wages and incomes policy, implemented through a process of centralised wage-bargaining and the institution of the social partnership; and fiscal consolidation, applied *ex ante* through public expenditure restraint. At the same time, structural policy initiatives have been undertaken to increase efficiency and competition in the economy through a programme of deregulation and increased international openness.

Structural adjustment has recently been accelerated by the establishment of the European Economic Area (EEA). As this agreement extends most of the provisions under the European Union's Single Market Programme to the EFTA countries (except Switzerland), participation constitutes for Austria the biggest step in structural reform the country has taken over the past decades. Thus, nearly all major remaining non-tariff barriers to merchandise trade are removed (mainly by harmonising norms and standards), financial and most other services are liberalised, free movement of labour is established and remaining restrictions on capital movements have been rescinded (including the acquisition of real estate)[18].

This chapter begins with a discussion of monetary and exchange rate policies. Whilst, like the rest of Europe, Austrian monetary policy was forced into a

Diagram 10. **INDICATORS OF ECONOMIC PERFORMANCE**
Average 1973-93[1]

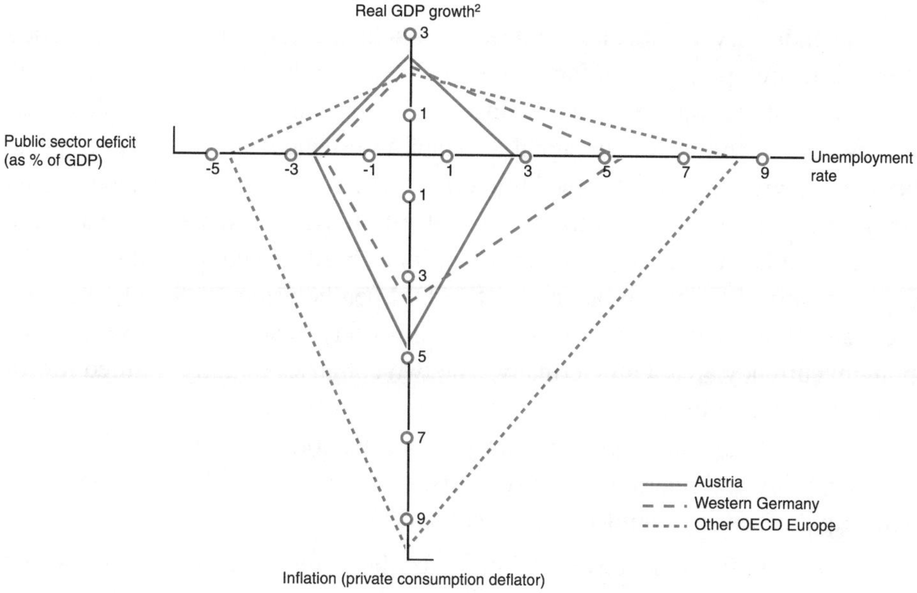

Real GDP growth[2]

Public sector deficit
(as % of GDP)

Unemployment
rate

Inflation (private consumption deflator)

——— Austria
— — · Western Germany
----- Other OECD Europe

1. 1993 estimated by OECD.
2. Standard deviations of respective growth rates as follows:
   Austria: 1.8
   Western Germany: 2.2
   Other OECD Europe: 1.7
Source: OECD, WIFO and Deutsche Bundesbank.

restrictive stance both prior to and in the early stages of the recession, largely as a result of developments in Germany, the credibility of the hard-currency policy has tended to insulate Austria from the exchange rate disruptions this policy tension induced elsewhere. It has even created some room for reducing short-term rates ahead of German rates. At the same time, the process of wage formation has required some modification, because of severe competitive pressures, while fiscal policy objectives have come under strain. The background to these two developments is discussed in subsequent sections of the chapter, prior to the presentation of the Secretariat's short-term projections.

Monetary and exchange rate policy

Success of the "hard currency option"

The monetary authorities adopted an exchange rate rule – the so-called "hard-currency option" – as far back as 1974, at the time of the first oil shock, when the schilling was revalued against the Deutschemark despite weak fundamentals. The intention was to signal a "stability-oriented" monetary policy and check wage growth over the medium-term.[19] The schilling was revalued again during 1979-81, in response to the second oil shock and since then has been pegged to the Deutschemark (Diagram 11). It has been argued, plausibly, that the definitive shift of exchange rate policy to a DM peg between 1979 and 1981 triggered an adjustment process which has ultimately made Austria part of an optimum currency area with Germany. The two countries initially fulfilled few of the necessary qualifications – the absence of asymmetric shocks and/or the presence of labour and capital mobility – but economic integration, increased wage flexibility and liberalised capital movements have created a situation where cyclical policy needs would normally coincide.[20]

German unification, however, imposed a large new asymmetric shock that led to painfully high interest rates and exchange rates, thus severely testing the credibility of the hard currency policy. However, Austria coped with these strains without abandoning its exchange rate peg against the Deutschemark. The currency turbulence of September 1992 and August 1993 left the Austrian schilling largely unscathed. With one minor exception, in August 1993,[21] there was no speculation against the Austrian schilling, so that it appears that the accumulated credibility of 20 years of hard currency policy has now been recognised by financial markets.

Indeed, the most striking feature of capital account developments since autumn 1992 has been a sizeable surplus in total long-term capital transactions, compared with a large deficit in 1991 and in the first three quarters of 1992 (Table 8). This turnaround reflected both relative return and portfolio risk factors, the latter being in turn evidence of confidence in the Austrian currency:

   i)   Portfolio investments by Austrians abroad fell significantly, reflecting not only better yields at home – i.e., a positive differential from German long term bond rates – but also greater aversion to foreign currency risk given large foreign-exchange losses in 1992;[22]

Diagram 11. **EXCHANGE RATE DEVELOPMENTS**

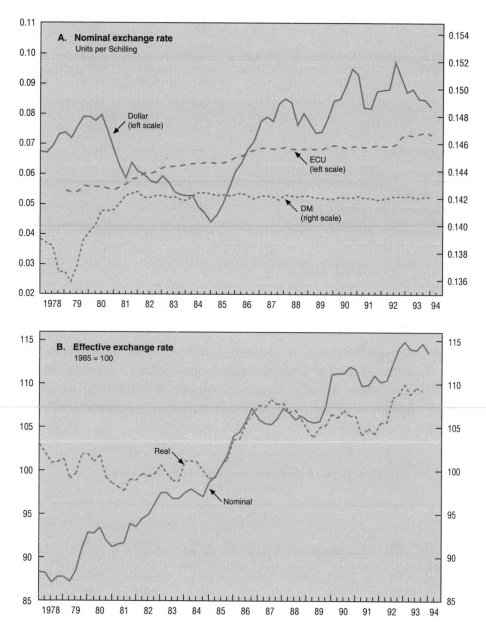

A. **Nominal exchange rate**
Units per Schilling

Dollar
(left scale)

ECU
(left scale)

DM
(right scale)

B. **Effective exchange rate**
1985 = 100

Real

Nominal

Source: OECD.

35

Table 8. The capital account

Billion schilling

	1989	1990	1991	1992	1993
Long-term capital, net [1]	6.1	−10.2	−24.4	7.8	75.8
Direct investment	−3.7	−11.6	−10.9	−10.3	−5.1
Outward	−11.3	−18.9	−15.0	−20.6	−16.3
Inward	7.7	7.4	4.2	10.3	11.2
Securities	19.9	15.5	13.1	37.7	99.9
Bank loans	−8.6	−28.0	−30.8	−13.6	1.0
Other	−1.5	13.9	4.1	−6.1	−20.0
Short-term capital, net [1]	10.5	8.9	24.8	13.2	−32.5
Net errors and omissions [1]	−8.4	−13.0	8.0	8.3	−6.1
Memorandum items:					
Change in central bank net foreign assets [2]	−11.6	+0.6	−9.2	−27.8	−26.6
Current account	+3.3	+13.6	0.8	−1.6	−10.6

1. Outflow −/Inflow +.
2. Increase −; decrease +; net of valuation changes (*i.e.* transactions only).
Source: Austrian National Bank, *Monthly Bulletin.*

ii) Foreign purchases of domestic securities rose substantially. This increased foreign demand seems to have reflected not only the yield differentials but also increased portfolio diversification demand by foreigners for narrow-band non-Deutschemark instruments.

Table 9. Austrian direct investment in Eastern Europe

In millions of schillings

	1989	1990	1991	1992	1993
Eastern Europe, total	766	4 780	5 936	4 988	5 646
(as a per cent of total DI outflow)	(6.8)	(25.3)	(39.6)	(24.3)	(39.8)
of which:					
Hungary	704	3 951	4 357	3 224	2 438
Czech Republic and Slovakia	19	165	1 038	1 407	2 440
Poland	12	42	274	152	123
Slovenia	..	..	..	139	517

Source: Austrian National Bank.

At the same time, direct foreign investment abroad by Austrian businesses continued to increase strongly, especially to eastern Europe (Table 9). However the main financial counterpart of the long-term portfolio inflow was a turnaround to huge short term capital outflow in 1993, from inflows in previous years. Most of these funds went to the purchase of short-term paper in Germany, where interest rates have been slightly higher.

Interest rate differentials and the term structure

Given the high mobility of international capital,[23] Austrian central bank policy consists of adjusting the interest rate differential with Germany in order to maintain the exchange rate peg.[24] Following trends in Germany, official interest rates have been gradually reduced since September 1992. By the end of March 1994, the discount rate had fallen from 8¼ to 5 per cent and the rate on short-term open market operations (GOMEX) from 9 to 5.5 per cent[25] – slightly exceeding the corresponding policy interest rate reductions in Germany. Hence, as a result of the enhanced credibility of the Austrian schilling, a negative short term interest rate differential opened up against Germany in September 1992, suggesting an unusual negative "country risk" premium against the anchor country.[26] This, in turn, helped to induce the huge short-term capital outflow to Germany noted above. Market rates declined in tandem, mainly at the short end, so that the earlier inversion of the yield curve was virtually eliminated (Diagram 12).

At the same time, the traditionally negative differential at the long-term end turned positive in mid-1991, as the German long-term interest rate began to decline, which, in combination with the increased confidence in the Austrian schilling, resulted in the above-noted boom in sales of schilling-denominated securities to non-residents.[27] The result has been that the term structure, which traditionally has been flatter than that of Germany, steepened considerably (in the sense that it became less inverted). This widening of the term structure gap relative to Germany may have reflected the fact that the expected decline in the Austrian short-term interest rate was smaller than that of the German short-term interest rate. However, a premium of about ¼ per cent on Austrian bonds relative to that on German bonds, as in February 1994, could be the normal result of higher capital market transaction costs, due to the thinness of Austrian markets.[28]

Diagram 12. **INTEREST RATE DEVELOPMENTS**

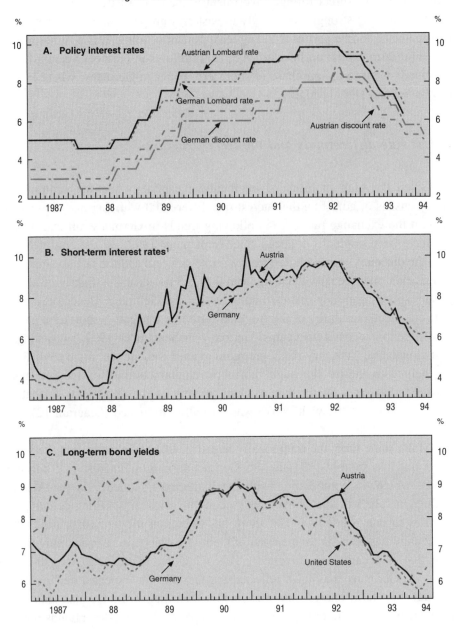

1. Call money.
Source: OECD, *Financial Statistics,* Austrian National Bank and Deutsche Bundesbank.

38

Money and credit expansion

These new patterns of interest rate differentials – lower short rates and a less inverted yield curve than in Germany and elsewhere – suggest a less restrictive stance of monetary policy than in Germany. Thus, monetary aggregates have been growing moderately, despite cyclically dampened demand for credit and portfolio shifts to non-monetary investments offering higher rates of interest.[29] In 1993, M3 grew by 4 per cent (compared with $4^{1}/_{4}$ per cent in 1992). Credit expansion over the same period weakened notably, to $3^{1}/_{2}$ per cent ($5^{1}/_{2}$ per cent one year earlier), given a sharp slowdown in the extension of credits to industry and trade. Issuing activity in the bond market, on the other hand, has been lively (implying an increase of more than 14 per cent in the outstanding stock), with the federal government and banks accounting for the lion's share. Domestic institutional investors and nonresidents were the main takers of these new issues.

Another factor which may have lessened the restrictive impact of monetary policy was the widespread, though declining, use of credit subsidies which dampen the interest sensitivity of domestic spending. As of end-1991, 24 per cent of direct domestic bank credits were subsidised in one form or another, compared with 28 per cent in 1988.[30] This change was more than accounted for by a significant decline in subsidised credits to industry, owing in part to the unwinding of subsidised credits to the nationalised industries, and suggesting a growing sensitivity of business investment demand to market rates. On the other hand, subsidisation of housing credits has expanded greatly (Table 10).

Despite the declining trend in subsidised credits to industry, there has been no thoroughgoing reform of the credit subsidy system. This has clearly negative consequences for public finances, while also causing distortions in the system of credit allocation by both banks and capital markets. In the first place, subsidised credits discourage competition between the banks; second, they may give rise to cross-subsidisation, in the form of larger margins on non-subsidised credits compensating for typically smaller margins on subsidised credits, with distorting effects on the domestic interest rate structure; and third, the large fixed costs of individual subsidised loans mean that a disproportionate share of such credits go to large enterprises, with small businesses being largely shut out. This also inhibits the development of the capital market, where large industry has little interest because of the easy access to cheap subsidised bank credit while small

Table 10. **Share of subsidised bank credits, by borrowing sector**[1]

	31 December 1988	31 December 1991	Difference in percentage points
	Share in per cent		
Industry and small-scale industry and crafts	39.9	29.9	−10.0
Industry	..	47.0	..
Small-scale industry and crafts	..	11.1	..
Trade	2.8	4.6	+1.8
Tourism	22.7	22.3	−0.4
Agriculture and forestry	13.3	11.9	−1.4
Transport and communications	34.2	10.0	−24.2
Housing associations	73.9	100.0	+26.1
Free professions	1.5	2.1	+0.6
Personal borrowers	21.1	9.8	−11.3
Other borrowers[2]	33.7	29.4	−4.3
Total = overall share of subsidised credits in total domestic banks' direct credits	28.2	23.8	−4.4

1. Sectoral shares of subsidised schilling bank credits in domestic banks' direct schilling credits, inclusive of Economic Recovery Programme credits extended by banks in trust.
2. Special state-owned companies (100 per cent subsidised), holding companies and others.
Source: Reports and Summaries of the Austrian National Bank, 2/1993.

businesses are denied access due to the existence of minimum qualifying requirements.

Wages and incomes policy

Reflecting the strong influence of corporatism, based on compulsory membership of the federal chambers of commerce or labour, as well as on a high degree of unionisation, wage formation in Austria is highly centralised and dominated by the social partner organisations. Centralisation and the close involvement of the social partners in the formulation of macroeconomic policy have, historically, combined to make for a high degree of wage responsiveness to cyclical developments, underpinning the exchange rate constraint. In the face of rising capacity slack, Austrian trade unions tend to be conscious of the danger of pricing labour out of the market. Over time, this attitude has been reflected in a marked degree of wage moderation, helping to keep relative unit labour costs in manufacturing on a downward trend, as well as to hold the unemployment rate low by international standards.

Collective wage agreements provide for broadly uniform pay increases across branches, geared to expected productivity gains and the rate of inflation in the overall economy. Effective-wage ("Ist-Lohn") clauses and supplementary agreements at the firm level, in turn, ensure flexible adjustment to the particular productivity and profit situation. However, since inter-sectoral labour mobility is traditionally low in Austria, such wage differentials have become entrenched and are actually among the highest in the OECD area. In this way, the structure of relative wages may fail to respond adequately to sectoral shifts in the supply and demand for labour.

While the centralised wage bargaining model has tended to work well in the past, promoting wage discipline and (in conjunction with the hard-currency policy) low inflation, it has recently come under critical review. The new international environment, including the opening up of the east, higher capital mobility, greater integration of markets, and the European currency devaluations, together with the world recession, have implied severe competitive pressures in the open sectors, which are largely price takers unable to pass through their rising labour costs. Under such circumstances, an incomes policy which is not geared to individual productivity performance may be inadequate to prevent competitive distortions. In particular, stubborn inflation in the sheltered sectors, which are better able to pass through these wage increases, leads to falling real incomes and exacerbates the competitiveness loss of the open sector insofar as it uses inputs from the sheltered sector. It also causes a misallocation of resources, as low-productivity jobs are preserved in the sheltered sectors, and encourages increased calls for protection, via an enlargement of the sheltered sector.

Against this background, the employers' side of the social partnership has called for a reorientation of incomes policy along the following lines:
- the collectively-agreed wage should be geared to productivity and price increases in the export sector, rather than in the overall economy;
- developments in the effective wage should reflect more flexibly the profit situations of individual firms;
- the social protection of incomes should be decoupled from the concept of the collective wage – i.e. low-skill workers should be permitted to work at less than "usual" Austrian wages (and trained), while minimum income levels should be maintained via social transfer mechanisms;

– measures should be taken to improve the efficiency of the sheltered/ public sectors, EU membership being important to promoting such reforms.

The unions for their part have been responsive to at least the first two of these proposals. The autumn 1993 wage agreements in heavy industry – which provide a signal for likely wage increases in the coming year for the overall economy – produced a collectively agreed wage increase of $2\frac{3}{4}$ per cent (compared with 4 per cent one year ago), substantially under the rate of nominal GDP growth per worker.[31] At the same time lower awards – in exchange for employment guarantees – are now possible for firms in financial difficulty, on a case by case basis, through the mechanism of an "opening clause". However, little use has as yet been made of such clauses.

In order to ensure that wage moderation in the 1993 wage round will feed through to decelerating inflation, thereby fostering price competitiveness and protecting real disposable incomes, the social partners initiated a "stability pact" in autumn 1993, which combined agreements on wages, prices and fees charges by banks and public utilities, as well as monetary and fiscal policy ingredients. Thus, the labour unions were called upon to settle for moderate wage increases while the increase in public tariffs and charges, usually occurring at the beginning of the year, were to be held to a ceiling of 3 per cent in 1994. However, the price and user-charge commitments have proved difficult to implement, given upward pressures on public utility and transport prices and problems in enforcing compliance both within the private sector (particularly the banks) and among the states and municipalities.

Fiscal policy

Budget developments in 1993 and 1994

The original federal budget proposal for 1993 envisaged a return to consolidation with a deficit on an administrative basis of Sch 60 billion (2.7 per cent of GDP). As economic prospects began to weaken, this was revised upward to Sch 64 billion (Table 11). The estimated outcome now shows a far higher deficit, at Sch 98.2 billion (4.7 per cent of GDP). This large overshoot reflects mainly the operation of the automatic stabilisers arising from the unexpected decline in

Table 11. **The Federal budget**

Schillings billion

	1991 Outturn	1992 Outturn	1993 Budget	1993 Preliminary outturn	1994 Budget voted
			Administrative basis		
Revenue					
Net taxes and contributions	385.6	426.2	449.7	430.4	460.9
Trading income [1]	84.8	89.4	93.2	90.2	63.1
Asset sales [2]	1.0	76.0	81.4	80.9	104.6
Other revenue	85.8				
Total revenue	557.2	591.6	624.3	601.5	628.6
(in per cent of GDP)	(29.2)	(29.0)	(29.1)	(28.6)	(28.6)
Expenditure					
Wages and salaries	137.7	146.5	153.4	155.5	133.8
Current expenditure on goods	60.5	61.7	67.3	61.8	67.1
Gross investment	25.4	26.8	28.2	26.0	24.9
Total spending on goods and services	223.6	235.0	248.9	243.3	225.8
Transfer payments [2]	278.1	299.1	317.7	330.1	367.3
Interest payments	76.1	81.4	88.2	85.3	86.2
Other expenditure	42.1	42.5	33.6	41.0	30.0
Total expenditure	619.9	658.0	688.4	699.7	709.3
(in per cent of GDP)	(32.5)	(32.3)	(32.1)	(33.2)	(32.2)
Net balance	−62.7	−66.3	−64.1	−98.2	−80.7
(in per cent of GDP)	(−3.3)	(−3.2)	(−3.0)	(−4.7)	(−3.7)
			Cash basis		
Revenue	510.6	559.2	590.0	562.3	586.1
Expenditure	585.0	618.6	658.9	666.8	681.7
Net balance	−74.4	−59.3	−68.9	−104.5	−95.6
(in per cent of GDP)	(−3.9)	(−2.9)	(−3.2)	(−5.0)	(−4.3)

1. Income from federal enterprises.
2. Including pensions to civil servants.
Source: Ministry of Finance.

economic activity. Federal government revenues from taxes (profit, sales, and trade taxes), federal railway earnings, and social security contributions all turned out lower than expected (by Sch 17½ billion), while spending on labour market measures was higher (Sch 7½ billion).

On top of the effects of the normal automatic stabilisers, utilisation of the second year of maternity leave benefits (introduced in the previous year) was markedly higher than anticipated, while privatisation receipts fell short of expectations. In February, the government introduced a "stabilisation package" of discretionary measures to revive the economy, but this contributed only a small amount to the overshoot. The most important was an increase in the business investment allowance from 20 to 30 per cent between 1 February 1993 and 31 March 1994. Other measures included some bringing forward of public investment and a widening of the limits on export credit guarantees. Finally, in 1993 the general household tax credit became graduated according to the number of children, while the single-earner tax credit was increased;[32] though this was partly paid for by elimination of other forms of family aid, disposable incomes still rose (by Sch 7 billion).

The administrative budget for 1994 provides for a sharp reduction in the deficit, to Sch 80.7 billion (3.7 per cent of GDP). This is despite an estimated Sch 17 billion net revenue loss due to tax reform (see below); a weak recovery (1½ per cent real and 4½ per cent nominal GDP growth); and recently expanded social benefits programmes. The main deficit reducing measures are as follows:

i)   The tax shortfall due to tax reform is to be made up by reserve drawdowns. Further, the mineral oil tax on petrol will be raised by 50 groschen per litre (parallel to a similar step in Germany), with part of these receipts going to the Länder (Länderzuschlag).[33] Unemployment insurance taxes will be raised by 0.7 per centage points, paid for in equal parts by employers and employees, to help finance labour market spending.

ii) Efforts will be made to contain the growth of social spending. Slower growth of pensions and related benefits will result from a new indexing method, based on the rate of increase in average wages *net* of social security contributions.[34] The federal government's liability share in pension insurance will be reduced (to 100 per cent).[35] There are also miscellaneous cuts in benefits and in civil service remunerations (such as overtime).

iii) Efficiency gains are expected from the decision to move the federal railways and the civil aeronautics board off-budget, as well as from the contracting out of labour market administration. Receipts from a resumption of sales under the privatisation programme are also anticipated.

The general government sector

The state and local governments are expected to show a collective surplus in both 1993 and 1994 – as they have in each year since 1989, after allowing for revenue-sharing (Part III). As of 1993, they will benefit substantially from the large increase (from 10 to 22 per cent) in the tax on interest earnings (the receipts from which they receive an above-average share). The social security system should continue to show approximately balanced accounts, with around 15 per cent of its receipts arising from federal budget transfers (Diagram 13).

Total general government expenditures are expected to keep rising in 1993-94 as a per centage of GDP, as they have since 1991 (Diagram 14).[36] The revenue ratio, which rose markedly between 1990 and 1992 and again in 1993, should remain broadly unchanged in 1994 despite tax reform. Thus, the total financial deficit, which had declined from 4¼ to 2 per cent of GDP between 1987 and 1992, is estimated to have risen to 3¼ per cent of GDP in 1993 and expected to increase further to 4 per cent in 1994. The outstanding debt of the

Diagram 13. **GOVERNMENT FINANCIAL BALANCES**[1]
In per cent of GDP

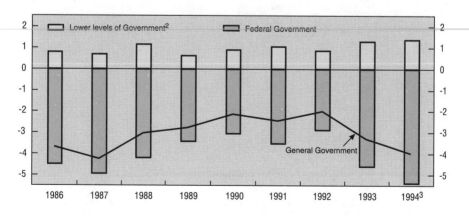

1. National accounts basis.
2. State and local governments, the chambers and social security funds.
3. Budgeted/Projected.
Source: Austrian Central Statistical Office and Ministry of Finance.

Diagram 14. COMPOSITION OF GENERAL GOVERNMENT EXPENDITURE AND REVENUE[1]

In per cent of GDP, cumulative

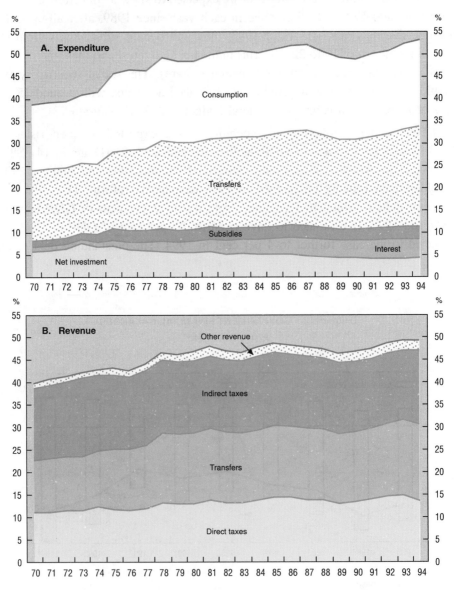

1. National accounts basis.

Source: OECD and Ministry of Finance.

Table 12. **The stance of fiscal policy**

Percentage of nominal GDP

	1987	1988	1989	1990	1991	1992	1993	1994
General government net lending	–4.3	–3.0	–2.8	–2.2	–2.5	–2.0	–3.3	–4.0
Change in general government net lending	–0.6	1.2	0.2	0.6	–0.3	0.4	–0.9	–0.9
of which:								
Due to automatic stabilisers	–0.3	1.0	0.4	0.8	0.0	–0.8	–1.5	–0.7
Change in structural balance	–0.3	0.2	–0.2	–0.2	–0.3	1.2	0.6	–0.2
Memorandum item:								
GDP-gap[1]	–2.3	–0.6	0.2	1.8	1.7	0.3	–2.4	–3.5

1. Difference between actual and potential GDP growth rates.
Source: OECD, *National Accounts*, and OECD calculations and projections.

public sector, however, should remain stable as a per cent of GDP, at around 60 per cent, as it has since 1989.

The structural component of the overall public sector deficit gives a clearer indication of the underlying stance of fiscal policy as well as of progress in budget consolidation which has been a major fiscal policy aim since 1986.[37] Between 1987 and 1991, fiscal stance was broadly neutral despite strong economic growth, suggesting that the government may have missed an opportunity to make greater headway in its medium-term deficit reduction plans (Table 12). In 1992, policy stance became more restrictive despite the onset of the economic downturn, the worsening in the deficit due to cyclical factors (automatic stabilisers) being more than offset by discretionary tightening among the states and municipalities. In general government terms, fiscal policy has thus been somewhat procyclical. In 1993 and 1994, the cyclical increase in the deficit is being fully reflected in the actual outturn, implying a reversion to a more neutral underlying stance.

The tax reform

The 1988-89 tax reform (*Economic Survey of Austria 1988/89*) focused on direct taxation and resulted in an alleviation of the tax burden on households and enterprises by cutting marginal tax rates substantially and widening the tax base. In addition, interest earnings were taxed more effectively. A second tranche of reforms has been envisaged since late 1990, the goals being *i)* the adaptation of

47

indirect taxes (VAT, consumption taxes) to EU norms; *ii)* greater ecological orientation of the tax structure; *iii)* a restructuring of business taxation to improve both profitability and financing ability; *iv)* correction for household "fiscal drag"; and *v)* simplification of tax regulations and administration.

Following a preliminary set of tax reform measures in 1992 and 1993 mainly geared to the environment and tax simplification,[38] the final and major stage of the current tax reform programme comes into operation in 1994. The main tax relief elements in that year are as follows:

- The general tax credit will be raised, while all wages and salaries under 11 500 schillings per month will be made tax-free. This corrects for fiscal drag since the 1989 tax reform, raising disposable incomes by about 1½ per cent.
- Capital tax and tax on industry and trade (Vermögens-, Gewerbesteuer) will be abolished – as will more minor business taxes. These tax cuts markedly improve the rate of return to capital, and also promote development of the capital market.
- New tax incentives will be established to strengthen the ability of businesses to issue equity, form partnerships, and borrow, and special benefits are given to small businesses.

At the same time, the following major business tax *increases* are being imposed:

- The corporate tax rate is being raised (from 30 to 34 per cent) and a minimum corporate tax payment introduced; also, various business tax loopholes will be eliminated. As of 1 April, the investment allowance will be permanently reduced to 15 per cent. These measures partially offset the benefits of the abolition of the profits and small-business taxes.[39]
- The current municipal payroll tax is being replaced by a general municipal charge on wages, which now encompasses all businesses (not just industry and trade), and at an increased rate (from 2 to 3 per cent). This implies a 70 to 75 per cent tax revenue increase for municipalities over the previous payroll tax.

Altogether, the tax reform measures implemented in 1994 imply a net reduction in the private sector's tax burden of Sch 17 billion – of which about Sch 4 billion accrues to firms (not all in the first year) and the remainder to households. An amount equivalent to around $\frac{1}{2}$ per cent of GDP will be added to the public sector budget deficit (slightly more in 1994), of which the bulk will be borne by the Federation.

In terms of medium-term economic effects, tax reform should boost real GDP by $\frac{1}{2}$ per cent ($\frac{1}{4}$ per cent in 1994), while increasing employment by about $\frac{1}{4}$ per cent (mostly after 1994), and raising the private consumption deflator by $\frac{1}{2}$ point ($\frac{1}{4}$ point in 1994).[40] The business tax environment will now be one of the most favourable in the OECD, rendering Austria more attractive as a locale for capital-intensive production. However, the increased municipal tax on wages will combine with the above-noted increase in unemployment insurance contributions to raise labour costs by almost 1 per cent,[41] having adverse effects on the labour market and perhaps accelerating the shift of labour-intensive production to eastern Europe. Indeed, whereas the gap with other European countries has been narrowed in the area of capital taxation, it has widened in the area of labour taxation. The rates of VAT and social security contributions also remain higher than in the average of EU countries, although the level of excise taxes is relatively low.

The short-term outlook

The projections to 1995: modest but accelerating recovery

Supported by the phasing in of the tax reforms and by falling short-term interest rates, the recovery should become more firmly established during 1994. However, the projected upturn in real GDP is expected to be only of the order of $1\frac{1}{2}$ per cent for 1994 as a whole (Table 13). This is broadly in line with the projection of the Austrian Institute of Economic Research (WIFO). The main restraining factor will be the continuing slow growth of European markets, accompanied by some loss in Austrian market share reflecting the lagged impact of real effective exchange rate appreciation. As a result, the recovery of business fixed investment will probably remain very weak. Though a stimulus to business investment should come from further interest rate cuts and corporate tax reform, the impact may, in both respects, take time to come through.

Table 13. **Economic projections to 1995**

Percentage change from previous year, constant 1983 prices

	1981-90 Average	1991	1992	1993[1]	1994[1]	1995[1]
Private consumption	2.5	2.4	1.8	1.0	1.6	2.5
Government consumption	1.3	2.6	2.4	2.1	2.0	1.0
Gross fixed investment	2.2	4.9	2.7	-2.6	0.5	3.3
Construction	1.8	5.7	5.4	0.4	1.9	2.5
Machinery and equipment	2.7	3.9	-0.7	-6.5	-1.5	4.6
Change in stocks[2]	-0.1	0.3	-0.4	-0.3	0.3	0.3
Total domestic demand	2.1	3.3	1.7	-0.0	1.7	2.8
Exports of goods and services	5.1	8.2	2.8	0.3	1.4	6.0
Imports of goods and services	4.7	8.9	2.8	1.0	1.8	6.6
Foreign balance[2]	0.1	-0.3	-0.0	-0.3	-0.2	-0.4
Gross domestic product	2.2	3.0	1.6	-0.4	1.5	2.4
Memorandum items:						
Private consumption deflator	3.6	3.4	3.8	3.7	2.8	2.3
GDP price deflator	3.8	3.4	4.2	3.7	2.8	2.4
Total employment	0.6	1.7	2.1	-0.7	-0.4	0.8
Unemployment rate[3]	3.3	3.5	3.6	4.2	4.6	4.8
Household savings ratio	10.4	13.4	11.8	11.4	11.8	11.6
Export market growth	4.7	2.6	-0.3	-4.7	3.2	6.0
Current balance ($US billion)	0.1	0.1	-0.3	0.2	0.3	0.4

1. OECD estimates and projections as of December 1993.
2. Change as a per cent of GDP in the previous period.
3. Standardised definition (microcensus).
Source: OECD and WIFO.

For most of 1994 personal sector demand will provide the main source of support for the recovery. Residential construction investment could remain relatively buoyant, judging from the level of construction orders in late 1993, while private consumption should continue to grow moderately. The effect of the planned tax reform, which mainly corrects for income bracket creep, together with lower inflation which is expected to fall below 3 per cent, will ensure a continued growth in real disposable income, albeit slow, in the face of further wage moderation and employment losses. As an immediate reaction to the net income gains from the tax reform, it is assumed that the savings ratio will go up by 1/2 percentage point, thereby offsetting the decline in 1993, although an increase in households' propensity to save beyond this appears unlikely.

In 1995, growth is expected to strengthen to around 2½ per cent, based mainly on a reversal of the main influences that were responsible for the recent recession:

i) Export market growth should pick up, while the effects of past export competitiveness losses will wane, permitting the Austrian share of world trade to stabilise. The assumptions behind this improvement are that wage moderation continues throughout the projection period and that exchange rates remain stable.[42]

ii) Business investment is assumed to respond positively to a number of influences: improved profits and sales expectations associated with wage moderation, renewed export optimism and continuing effects of tax reform; the cumulating lagged effect of past interest rate declines and a normalised yield curve; prospective EU membership and the need for rationalisation investments designed to meet intensifying international competition from the newly cost-competitive countries of western Europe, as well as from the dynamic economies of the far east and from the low-wage countries of eastern Europe.

These trends imply a potential narrowing of the trade deficit over the medium term. This is because rationalisation investments should ensure that Austria catches up with other OECD countries in terms of the skill and techno-logical levels embodied in its productive structures, in turn strengthening the underlying competitive position of industry. This outcome is highly contingent, however, on the avoidance of further restrictive trade measures against eastern European and other developing country goods exports.[43] A narrowing in the trade deficit is all the more desirable insofar as further expansion of tourism exports – which traditionally covered the growing trade deficit – may be constrained by capacity-limiting factors (such as environmental goals).

Risks to the projection

The outlook is subject to considerable risks because of international uncer-tainties, which may mean a weaker outturn for exports. First, growth in Germany and other European economies may be slower than projected. Second, German interest rates could be slower to come down than expected (though the combina-tion of slower German growth and slower interest rate cuts would seem unlikely).

Third, further disturbances in the ERM, especially in the event of interest rates failing to decline as fast as expected, could imply renewed upward pressure on the schilling.[44] Together with the possibility that a failure to tackle existing impediments to competition could result in slower than expected progress on disinflation, this could have adverse consequences for the real exchange rate and hence for international competitiveness. On the other hand, lower interest rates and an improving business climate, perhaps related to the final approach to EU membership, might increase the confidence of investors and households more than expected.

III. Public sector issues

The OECD last examined the Austrian public sector in 1989, following the implementation of a major income tax reform and at a time when the role of the public sector was being reappraised in the context of a restructuring of the nationalised industries. The principal priority then identified was the need to carry through the announced medium-term programme of fiscal consolidation, aimed at cutting the federal budget deficit/GDP ratio from 5 per cent of GDP in 1986 to 2½ per cent by 1992. This switch towards consolidation succeeded in stabilising deficit in absolute terms and, benefiting from an extended period of buoyant growth, in gradually reducing it as a proportion of GDP. By 1992, while missing the original target, the federal deficit ratio had come down to 3¼ per cent and the primary balance had moved into surplus. Including the budgets of other government levels and public sector agencies the general government deficit had fallen to a low of 2 per cent and the rise in public sector debt had levelled-off at around 57 per cent of GDP. On both accounts, the Austrian budgetary situation compared favourably with that of other OECD economies (Table 14).

More recently, the consolidation process has stalled and is even being reversed. While the recession is partly responsible, there also appear to be a number of structural factors at work which are still making for upward pressure on public expenditure and budget deficits. Some of these pressures are shared with other OECD economies, with similar deleterious implications for allocative efficiency, distribution and budget flexibility. Moreover, certain institutional features may have led to additional problems of lack of transparency and defective control. These have been related, in particular, to the relationships between the various levels of government, which have blurred financial accountability by separating spending from financing responsibilities. They also relate, more generally, to the difficulties of managing the complex of government and semi-government agencies, which have led to a lack of clarity in setting policy goals

53

Table 14. **Public sector balance and debt/GDP ratios in the OECD area, 1992** [1]

Per cent of GDP

Countries	Public sector	Debt ratios
Austria	**–2.5**	**56.6**
United States	–3.8	61.3
Japan	0.9	67.9
Germany	–3.3	43.6
France	–4.0	52.4
Italy	–9.8	108.7
United Kingdom	–5.7	41.1
Belgium	–6.8	137.2
Denmark	–3.0	63.1
Netherlands	–3.4	78.4
Norway	–2.1	43.6
Spain	–5.6	52.7
Sweden	–7.7	55.4
OECD Europe	–5.4	62.8
OECD Total	–3.8	63.1

1. General government, including Social security.
Source: OECD, *Economic Outlook No. 54.*

and the absence of incentives to cost-effective management (Table 15). These problems raise questions both about the proper design of fiscal institutions in a federal state and the best means of ensuring greater efficiency in the provision of public services.

The chapter begins with a discussion of medium-term budgetary pressures. This is followed by an analysis of institutional factors, concentrating first on the issue of the Austrian federal structure ("fiscal federalism") and then on financial relations with other public agencies. On both aspects, problems are highlighted by a number of case studies in public sector efficiency and resource allocation. The final section of the chapter outlines the steps being taken to improve budgetary control and responsibility and the further reforms needed to cope with the rising medium-term pressure on Austrian public finances.

Table 15. **The size of the public sector in OECD countries**[1]

Countries	General government outlays	General government receipts
	Per cent of nominal GDP	
Austria	**50.9**	**48.5**
United States	34.6	30.7
Japan	32.6	33.5
Germany	49.4	46.2
France	52.2	48.2
Italy	53.9	44.0
United Kingdom	43.0	37.3
Belgium	50.8	44.1
Denmark	60.2	57.2
Netherlands	55.2	51.8
Norway	56.8	54.7
Spain	44.9	39.3
Sweden	66.9	59.3
OECD Europe	50.4	45.0
OECD total	41.2	37.4

1. Average 1991-93.
Source: OECD, *Economic Outlook No. 54.*

Medium-term pressures and the need for reform

Underlying fiscal disequilibrium

As the analysis in the previous chapter has shown, central government finances have weakened recently, with federal government net lending now diverging significantly from the medium-term consolidation path laid down in the late 1980s (Diagram 15). While a significant part of the deviation is due to weak overall activity and the Austrian structural budget situation is not worse than the OECD average, it is apparent that the drive for consolidation had already stalled before the onset of the current recession. Indeed, the opportunity offered by the boom to proceed decisively towards major deficit reduction was to a large extent missed (see Part II).[45] Thus, by early 1991, when economic activity had just attained its peak, the government had postponed the target of a 2½ per cent

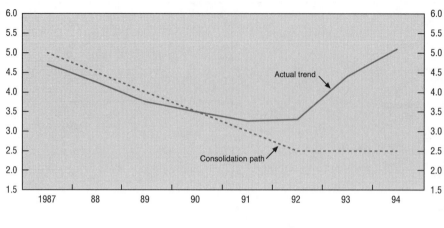

1. Administrative basis.
Source: Ministry of Finance.

deficit/GDP ratio from 1992 to 1994. Moreover, the focus of deficit reduction had shifted away from the expenditure to the revenue side, contrary to original intentions. Despite the 1989 tax cut the ratio of federal government tax receipts to GDP has been allowed to rise by 2 per centage points over the last five years, with federal expenditure keeping pace.

In terms of the general government account, the ratios of expenditure and revenues to GDP rose by 3 per centage points between 1988 and 1993, while overall government net lending remained in the range of 2 to 3 per cent of GDP (Diagram 16). This was low enough for the gross public debt ratio to stabilise. Moreover, budget deficits have at no time posed any problem of financing. However, medium-term projections suggest that, based on current legislation, the central government deficit is set to remain close to 5 per cent of GDP until 1996 and that the ratio of public debt will rise above 60 per cent.[46] Having been one of the few countries to be able to fulfil the Maastricht criteria, Austria now appears to need further fiscal action in order to reverse the trend towards divergence (Diagram 17).

Diagram 16. GROWING PUBLIC SECTOR
Per cent of GDP

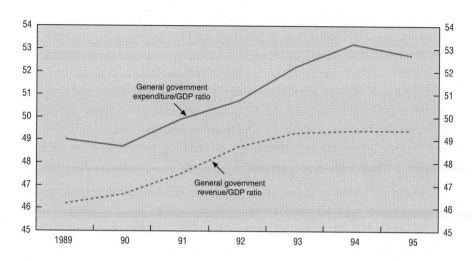

Source: OECD, *Economic Outlook* No. 54, December 1993.

Diagram 17. GENERAL GOVERNMENT DEFICIT AND DEBT
Per cent of GDP

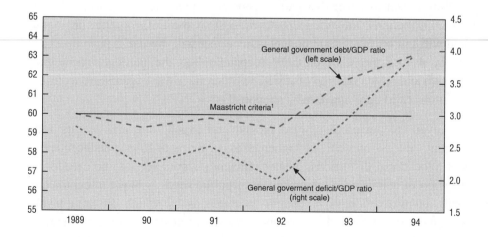

1. 3% of GDP for the deficit and 60% of GDP for the debt.
Source: Ministry of Finance.

Pressures on public spending

Moreover, over the longer run, pressures making for greater imbalances are likely to increase beyond those implied by current policy settings. Prospective EU membership will itself require a substantial annual net contribution. Legal commitments made in recent years, mainly in the area of social transfers and debt servicing for off-budget agencies, have as yet not had their full impact on government outlays. Thus, the OECD medium-term projections suggest that, even under favourable growth assumptions, additional fiscal action may be needed to bring down general government net lending and contain the public debt ratio in the second half of the decade.[47]

Looking still further ahead, the ageing population will constitute a rapidly rising burden on public finances (see *Economic Survey of Austria, 1988/89*). While, compared with other countries, the demographic structure is already biased towards the elderly, birth rates are among the lowest in the OECD area. Therefore, the share of people aged 60 years and above in the total population is set to rise from one-fifth to almost one-third over the next three-and-a-half decades (Diagram 18). The problem is further exacerbated by the fact that retirement benefits are relatively generous and the average effective retirement age has fallen to a low of 58 years. Since the federal government has taken on a legal obligation to cover that part of pension expenditure not covered by insurance contributions, the full incremental cost of the unfavourable demographic trend will fall on the federal budget. This effect will, by itself, push up expenditure by 4 to 8 per cent of GDP (depending on the particular demographic scenario) and only a fraction of it will be offset by lower expenditure required for education, child care and family support.[48]

Given the persistent upward pressure on expenditure and deficits and the potential "excess burden" of higher taxes, in terms of labour disincentives and other allocational distortions, greater efficiency would seem to be needed in the allocation of resources if the provision of public services is not to contract. This entails an overhaul both of control mechanisms by which different levels of government interact to achieve public expenditure goals and a reconsideration of the scope. In Austria's case, defects in these two areas may have led to over-spending and resource misallocation. Two broad aspects of public management are particularly at issue:

Diagram 18. **THE AGEING POPULATION**

Per cent of total population

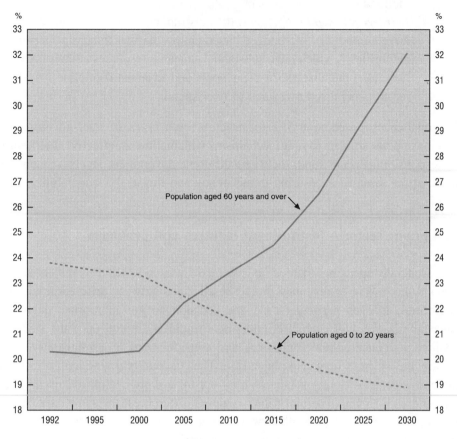

Source: Statistisches Jahrbuch fuer die Republik Östereich, 1993.

-   *"Fiscal federalism"*: the efficiency benefits of decentralised spending, which derive from an ability of regional and local levels of government to identify needs and preferences may provide a public choice rationale for a federal government system. Decentralisation, however, needs to be accompanied by financial discipline on local or regional government spending that appear to be somewhat deficient in some parts of the

Austrian public sector; otherwise, inherent benefits may be offset by ineffective cost management.

- *Extra-governmental agencies*: the Austrian public sector is made up of a large number of "off-budget" legal entities besides the basic "territorial authorities", which have substantial financial resources at their disposal. Here also the absence of clear goals and financial discipline may have led to generalised pressures to over-spend.

The challenges posed in trying to structure both types of inter-governmental relationship are similar: to find mechanisms which allow an effective distribution of responsibilities and funds between different government levels and entities while at the same time ensuring transparency and financial accountability.

The public sector – institutional features and problems

Generally speaking, there is no "optimal" way in which government spending and the raising of revenues should be allocated between different levels and authorities. In each particular case, the decision on the appropriate degree of (de)centralisation will, apart from historical tradition, depend upon the size of a country, its constitutional framework and considerations of administrative efficiency. Policy goals may also play a role. Thus, a country giving high priority to the convergence of living standards may opt for a more centralised fiscal structure allowing an equalisation of inter-regional differences; the same may be true for countries with a highly developed social welfare system. Given a constitutionally-imposed federal structure, as in Austria, there is an *a priori* case for fiscal arrangements to reflect the sharing of responsibilities between different government levels. However, the benefits of regional and local autonomy have to be set against potential disadvantages in terms of efficiency in the collection of revenues or of the overall distribution of welfare.

"Fiscal federalism" in Austria

Austria is a federal state where government responsibilities are shared between three levels of territorial authority, the federation (Bund), the nine federal states (Länder) and the municipalities (Gemeinden). Furthermore, the public sector comprises a number of other legal entities which carry out govern-

Table 16. **Gross public expenditure by government level**

Per cent of total

	Federal government [1]	States [2]	Municipalities [3]	Chambers	Social security	Total
1960	63.8	7.5	8.8	2.1	17.8	100.0
1970	49.2	10.2	18.4	1.8	20.4	100.0
1980	46.5	12.8	17.4	1.5	21.8	100.0
1990	48.7	11.8	15.5	1.7	22.3	100.0
1993	47.7	11.6	16.6	1.5	22.6	100.0
1993 (Sch billion)	822.2	200.5	285.4	25.0	389.0	1 722.1

1. Including federal government funds.
2. Excluding Vienna.
3. Including Vienna.
Source: Austrian Ministry of Finance.

mental functions – like the professional organisations (Chambers), the social security bodies and the public funds, such as the Family Benefit Fund or the Hospital Co-operation Fund (Table 16). The distribution of major government responsibilities between the Bund and the Länder is determined by the constitution. This distribution, however, is not straightforward, and a distinction is made between legislative and administrative responsibilities. While the most important national agenda – like defence, foreign policy, macroeconomic management, etc. – are assigned wholly to the Bund, and others of mainly regional and local importance – like construction laws and regulations – entirely to the states, responsibilities are shared between the two levels in other matters – like trade and industry, water supply, regulations concerning motor vehicles – in the sense that the Bund is responsible for legislation and the states for administration.[49] A general clause gives the states responsibility for all matters not mentioned by the constitution.

Revenue-sharing under the federal system

Although the constitution provides for the sharing of government responsibilities between three levels of territorial authorities, the right to levy taxes is concentrated with the Bund. Overall, 74 per cent of gross revenues (including social security contributions) go to the central government in Austria, by far the highest ratio among federal countries [the range for gross revenues elsewhere

Table 17. **Federal revenue and expenditure structures – an international comparison**

Per cent

	Share of total expenditure [1]			Share of total revenue [1]			Share of intra-governmental transfers in total revenue	
	C	R	L	C	R	L	R	L
Austria	**70**	**14**	**17**	**65**	**17**	**19**	**42**	**17**
Germany	60	22	18	61	21	18	15	28
Canada	42	40	18	39	41	20	19	45
Switzerland	48	28	24	49	27	24	26	16
United States	59	18	23	53	21	26	20	37
Denmark	45	–	55	49	–	51	–	42
France	81	–	17	82	–	18	–	35
Italy	72	–	28	67	–	33	–	81

Note: C = central government; R = regional; L = local.
1. Net of intra-governmental transfers.
Source: Economic and Social Advisory Board, *op. cit.*, Vienna 1992.

being from 64 per cent in Germany to 50 per cent in Canada] (Table 17). Conversely, the states and municipalities can rely only to a small extent on "own" revenue sources to finance their legal commitments and other tasks and assignments. Such "own" revenues account for 17 per cent of current total revenues for the municipalities and less than 3 per cent for the states.[50] Consequently, almost the whole of state revenues (and 30 per cent for the municipalities) are accounted for by revenues received from the federation (Table 18). These consist – for the states in roughly equal amount – either of fixed shares of the major revenues collected centrally, or of transfers, including those earmarked for specific responsibilities carried out by the states, like compulsory education or housing.

As a result of the revenue sharing process, which is highly complex,[51] the proportion of their gross revenues which the states can spend at their own discretion is raised to about 40 per cent. In other federal countries, the intermediate government level's independent resources account for between 55 per cent (United States) and 72 per cent (Germany), so the degree of "self-financing" is in this respect quite low in Austria. The municipalities, on the other hand, have

Table 18. **Revenue structure of States and Communities**

Per cent of total revenues, 1989

	States[1]	Communities[2]
Own taxes	2.4	17.3
Federal revenue shares	45.8	22.0
Transfers from other government levels	46.9[3]	8.4
Public charges	–	6.3
Debt raised	2.7	4.3
Other revenues[4]	2.2	41.7
Total	**100.0**	**100.0**

1. Including Vienna as a federal province.
2. Including Vienna as a community.
3. For example, earmarked transfers for housing subsidies, cost defrayal for teachers' salaries, community contribution to provinces ("Landesumlage").
4. For example, drawing on reserves, privatisation and other one-off revenues; for communities also certain user charges.
Source: Economic and Social Advisory Board, *op. cit.*, Vienna 1992.

54 per cent of their revenues coming from "own" taxes and central revenue shares – a higher ratio than for any other federal country (Tables 19 and 20).

Spending responsibilities and the transfer system

Gross public expenditure is also concentrated in the hands of the central government to a much higher degree in Austria than in any other federal country (78 per cent compared with a range of 50 per cent in Canada to 65 per cent in the United States). Part of this is explained by the relatively substantial amount of transfers paid by the Bund to the lower levels of government (Table 21). However, even adjusted for these transfers the central government share in overall net expenditure remains highest in Austria, with nearly 70 per cent. It is barely higher in some "centralised" countries (Italy 72 per cent) and can even be considerably lower (Denmark 45 per cent). This dominance is mainly at the expense of the states, whose share in gross expenditure (15 per cent) is clearly lower than that of any intermediate level in other countries (ranging from 27 per cent in the United States to 48 per cent in Canada). The expenditure share of the municipalities is also relatively low, but, again, closer to the position obtaining in other federal systems. The dominant role of the Bund is thus mainly at the expense of the states, whereas the municipalities have a degree of financial autonomy similar to those in other federal countries.

Table 19. **The distribution of government revenues**

Stage 1   Revenue sharing

Joint federal tax revenues ("gemeinschaftliche Bundesabgaben")
    minus tax refunds ("Erstattungen", z. B. Bausparprämien)
Budgeted gross revenues (Steuereinnahmen lt. Bundeshaushalt)
    minus *a-priori* deductions ("Abgeltungsbeträge", z. B. FLAG)
Revenues to be shared between territorial authorities
    − Vertical sharing
        Fixed proportions (different from each tax)
    − Horizontal sharing
        Among Länder and communities
        Criteria:
            Local tax yield (= 20 per cent of revenues)
            Population size (= 80 per cent of revenues)

Stage 2   Transfers

Earmarked transfers (*e.g.* housing subsidies) ["Zweckzuschüsse"]
Cost defrayals (*e.g.* teacher salaries) ["Kostenübernahmen"]
Grants-in-aid (*e.g.* for major investment, to restore budget equilibrium)
["Finanzzuweisungen"] financed out of 13.5 per cent of Gemeinde revenue shares retained
by the Länder.
Community contribution to Länder ["Landesumlage"] (8.3 per cent of Gemeinde revenues).

Stage 3   Implicit financial flows

Induced by:
    Transfers to other government agencies (*e.g.* public funds)
    Changes in tax laws and tax rates
    Private sector activities of public authorities.

The transfer procedure on the lower government levels is guided in the main by two principles: productivity, based on regional or local tax revenues, and the demographic principle, based on the number of inhabitants. About 80 per cent of municipal resources are distributed according to population size. Thus, the states have very little responsibility for providing their own financial resources.[52]

Implications for efficiency

As the above description shows, the Austrian federal system is based on a complex, revenue-sharing system which gives rise to a number of problems and distortions:

Table 20. The sharing of joint federal revenues, 1994

Per cent shares of total revenue by tax

Tax	Estimated revenue	of which going to:		
		Federal government	Provinces	Communities
	Sch billion	In per cent		
Taxes on income and property	181.4	58.8	22.5	18.6
of which:				
Income tax	30.7	48.6	27.4	24.0
Wage tax	123.5	63.2	20.6	16.2
Capital gains tax	2.6	19.9	13.3	66.8
Interest income tax	23.0	53.0	27.0	20.0
Inheritance and gift tax	1.5	70.0	30.0	–
Other taxes	234.4	68.9	18.5	12.6
of which:				
Value-added tax	193.7	69.4	18.8	11.8
Mineral oil tax	23.9	88.6	8.6	2.8
Real estate tax	5.0	4.0	–	96.0
Motor car taxes	7.2	50.0	50.0	–
Beverage taxes	3.3	38.6	33.9	27.5
Total tax revenues	415.9	64.5	20.3	15.2

Source: Austrian Ministry of Finance.

Table 21. Transfers between public authorities

Sch million, 1989

Transfers to:	Transfers from:						
	Federal government	Provinces	Communities	Social security	Chambers	Funds	Total
Bund	0	1 331	295	380	23	261	2 290
Länder	53 165	56	7 785	0	0	4 225	65 231
Gemeinden	3 239	5 284	2 948	0	0	3 803	15 274
Social security	60 667	54	2	13 551	63	136	74 473
Chambers	858	1 277	8	8	0	0	2 151
Funds	14 641	3 515	313	4 090	16	810	23 385
Total	132 570	11 517	11 351	18 029	102	9 235	182 804

Source: Economic and Social Advisory Board, *op. cit.*, Vienna 1992.

- The automatic earmarking of funds from particular revenue sources to certain spending categories creates upward pressure on spending in the categories linked to revenue sources which have trended upward fairly steadily over time (for example, the more income elastic revenue sources). Thus, spending may well increase even as the underlying need for services decreases, as is the case in family allowances and housing subsidies;
- The fact that the share of overall tax revenues eventually transferred to the states and the municipalities is determined by criteria which largely emphasise size of population, and even "need", contributes towards an equal supply of public services nationwide. On the other hand, it implies a lack of incentive for states and communities to improve the quality of their local tax base. Thus, for example, local governments have little incentive to accept projects that may involve some negative externalities for local residents (*e.g.* airports, waste disposal sites, other transport facilities) but which might at the same time increase the tax base;
- The rise of federal transfers for the automatic defrayal of costs, combined with the assignment of responsibilities for spending decisions to lower levels of government, creates a strong bias towards over-supply;
- The reliance of categorical grants in aid (*e.g.* for major investments) rather than block grants leaves little room for local choice.

More generally, since the overwhelming part of the legal responsibilities assigned to the states by the federal constitution is financed from sources outside the states' responsibility, there is no direct connection between the political responsibilities of spending and taxing. Popular spending decisions are in many instances taken at the lower government level closer to the electorate, while unpopular taxing decisions are taken at the more distant central level. This separation creates distortions in the supply of public services. Local and regional populations will tend to claim more public services which they regard as "free" in the sense of obtaining a higher share of a given quantity (supplied at the national level). Local and regional governments will be tempted to bow to these claims or even take the initiative in increasing supply as the cost will be borne by the central level.

This tendency to oversupply will be particularly strong for expenditure financed by earmarked transfers from the Bund. Whereas there is an incentive to apply efficiency criteria for public services provided by the states from general revenue shares – as higher outlays on one item will mean lower ones on others – no such incentive exists for items financed by earmarked resources. Such financial arrangements exist for housing subsidies and education costs. For these areas there is empirical evidence of inefficiencies and over-supply by international standards.[53]

Two case studies: education and housing

• Education

By long tradition the Bund bears the costs of salaries and retirement benefits of the teachers employed by the states. In all, in 1993 these refunds amounted to some 7 per cent of all government revenues. Since the early 1980s expenditure on this item has broadly kept pace with the overall trend in spending, despite the relief provided by demographic trends: as a consequence of the falling birth-rate, the number of children of compulsory school age has fallen by more than 25 per cent since the early 1970s. Given the policy priority granted to education up to the mid-1970s and the long lags involved in teacher training, an excess supply of teachers built up during the 1980s. At least part of the surplus was absorbed by lowering class size and the pupil/teacher ratio[54] (Table 22). The states, responsible for providing compulsory education, but not for bearing personnel costs, had a strong incentive to boost the employment of teachers, particularly as such policy could be defended in terms of improving the "quality of education".

The fact that the federal government covers personnel costs is logical inasmuch its makes decisions in such areas as curriculum, class size, teaching loads and teaching standards. However, the education guidelines established by the federal government are, perhaps necessarily, vague (*e.g.* the guidelines may specify that class size may not be more than 30 students, but it can be significantly less). In a system of automatic cost defrayal by the federal government for local expenses, the vagueness of the guidelines permits local demand for educational services to become inflated. At the same time, decisions taken at the federal level have financial implications for municipal governments, which are responsible for providing material infrastructure (buildings, classroom facilities, equipment). For the sake of the accountability and effectiveness of the system as a whole, it would be desirable if legal and financial responsibilities in educational

Table 22. **Indicators of education trends**

Annual averages 1980-92, percentage change

	Compulsory general	Vocational education	Secondary education	Total primary/ secondary	Higher education
Enrolment	−2.15	−1.99	0.35	−1.59	5.25
Teachers	1.03	−0.55	2.17	1.33	3.57
Pupil-teacher ratio	−3.15	−1.45	−1.78	−2.88	1.62
Real expenditure per student (1983 prices)	3.37	1.60	2.42	3.25	−0.51
Memorandum item:					
Pupil/teacher ratio					
1980	13.9	57.3	8.9	14.5	13.8
1992	9.5	48.1	7.2	10.2	16.8

Source: Submission by the Ministry of Finance.

matters were concentrated on the same level of government. Indeed, this level of government may differ for different levels or types of education.

- Housing

While construction laws and regulations and residential building are a legal responsibility of the states, the federal government has always been responsible for housing promotion and related subsidy schemes. Before 1988, a fixed proportion (10.19 per cent) of direct tax revenues was earmarked for housing subsidies. In 1988, legal responsibility for housing promotion was transferred from the federation to the states, each of which passed its own law regulating the matter for its own territory. However, financial responsibility remains with the Bund, the change being effectively an accounting one.[55]

Since the resources earmarked for housing promotion come from relatively "elastic" taxes the sector is guaranteed a comfortably growing supply of funds. The states and the municipalities thus have no constraint on spending the resources available, which serve to guarantee incomes to local construction firms and attract residents and (thus) taxpayers. At the same time, studies have shown that housing subsidies in Austria are not only generous but also tend to favour the middle and upper income strata.[56]

In view of the change in legislation which took place in 1988, it is regrettable that the occasion was missed to strengthen financial autonomy and responsibility of the states by abolishing the earmaking of revenue shares for housing subsidies.[57] This would have provided an incentive for reviewing the efficiency of housing promotion, leading potentially to a general lowering of subsidies and the phasing out of market distortions.

Managing public agencies

Apart from the territorial authorities, there are a number of other "para-fiscal" institutions which to some extent carry out government responsibilities and are therefore part of the public sector; among these are the social security institutions, the professional associations (chambers), public funds as well as a number of public enterprises like the Post and Telecommunication Administration (ÖPT) or the Austrian Federal Railways (ÖBB). Their governmental function is reflected, *inter alia* in their legal status, their mandates and tasks assigned. They are financed either by user charges – in the case of public enterprises – or by compulsory (social insurance) contributions and (membership) fees as well as by transfers from the federal budget.

Their financing, particularly the part involving the federal government, gives rise, in some instances, to problems similar to those discussed under the heading of fiscal federalism. Institutional arrangements are such that inherent pressure for rising expenditure may be exerted on the federal budget, making for a "structural" widening of the deficit. Such pressure may arise from a number of sources: because goals for public intervention and federal financial contributions are unclearly defined; because decisions on services offered are separated from responsibilities for their financing; from automatic access to government funds and thus the lack of incentive for cost-effective management; and from a disregard of the long-term implications of policy decisions. These problems may be illustrated by a number of examples.

The Federal railways

As in many western European countries, the Austrian Federal Railways (ÖBB) have by tradition been a public enterprise, with the Bund, as the owner, responsible for maintenance and investment. It also pays substantial transfers to cover operational and debt service cost, amounting to more than 5 per cent of overall Federal expenditure in 1993. These transfers cover retirement pensions; revenue losses due to services rendered in the general public interest through subsidised fares and tariffs; maintenance of unprofitable lines; offering of short-distance public transport, etc., and other operational losses (Table 23).

Table 23. **Federal government transfers to the Federal Railways (ÖBB)**
Sch million, 1991

Old-age pensions	12 693
Granting of "social fares"	3 441
Granting of subsidised tariffs	1 520
Road transportation fee	54
Continuation of low-frequency lines	2 022
Personal commuter transport	3 449
Maintenance of railroad infrastructure	4 735
Total	27 914

Source: *Annual Statement of ÖBB,* 1991

Over the last 30 years, the "self-financing" ratio of the ÖBB has fallen steadily from over 80 per cent to less than 50 per cent (Diagram 19). Operational revenues have been dampened by the loss of market shares *vis-à-vis* road transportation, the extension of "social" fares and the flattening trend of overall economic activity. Expenditure, on the other hand, has risen much faster, due to the widening and improvement of services offered in order to remain "competitive" and to relatively modest cuts in personnel.

By international comparison, labour productivity within the ÖBB appears to be quite low. In terms of output per employee in 1990 it was 27 per cent below the level of Deutsche Bundesbahn (DB) and 36 per cent below that of the Swiss Bundesbahn (SBB). In terms of revenues, excluding refunds, the difference is even more striking: revenues per employee of the ÖBB were only 57 per cent of those of DB and 38 per cent compared with the SBB figure (Table 24). Indeed, while operational revenues covered as much as 75 per cent of total outlays of SBB and 62 per cent at DB, the corresponding figure for the ÖBB was only 48 per cent in 1990.[58] At the same time, traffic density (service kilometres per rail kilometre) has been nearly as high for ÖBB as for DB.

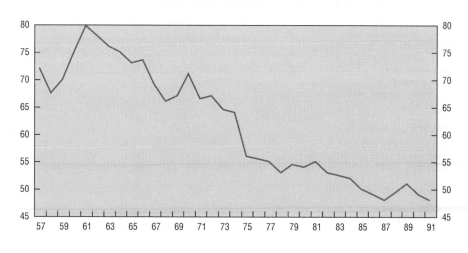

Source: Puwein 1992, *op. cit.*

Manning at ÖBB is still at a high level, despite a reduction by 10 per cent over the last 20 years, in contrast to DB, which succeeded in raising output per employee by no less than 77 per cent over the last fifteen years, to a large extent by cutting personnel by more than 40 per cent. Although salaries are relatively low, particularly in the early stages of service, given the relatively low productivity unit personnel costs are markedly higher for ÖBB than for the two other national railway companies. Procurement costs too are relatively high as the investment and procurement policy of ÖBB has been geared towards securing jobs in Austrian industry.

The low profitability of ÖBB is also caused by relatively low passenger fares determined by social and environmental considerations.[59] However, it is doubtful how far the envisaged goals are actually attained. Empirical evidence on redistributive effects shows for Germany and Austria that low fares benefit primarily middle-income strata rather than low-income people.[60] Moreover, despite a considerable price advantage in favour of rail, there has been relatively little shift from road to rail traffic.[61] Although train fares in Switzerland are one-

71

Table 24. **Performance indicators of national railway companies of Austria, Germany and Switzerland, 1990**

	ÖBB[1]	DB[2]	SBB[3]
Operational structure			
Average transportation distance (km)			
Personal transport	38	41	42
Goods transport	199	222	160
Traffic density per railroad kilometre (million			
unit per km)	3.8	3.9	6.5
Productivity (per employee)			
Transport volume (1 000 units))[4]	4.9	5.8	9.0
Transport output (million units per km)	343	466	553
Revenues (Sch 1 000)	343	561	851
Costs (Sch per unit/km)			
Personnel	1.54	1.35	1.27
Material and depreciation	0.54	0.60	0.78
Total operational costs	1.80	1.67	1.66
Personnel cost per employee (Sch 1 000)	529	627	704
Receipts from fares			
Sch per per/km	0.59	0.88	1.05
Sch per net ton/km	0.84	0.96	1.27
Sch per unit/km	0.73	0.93	1.15

1. Austrian Federal Railways (Österreichische Bundesbahn).
2. German Federal Railways (Deutsche Bundesbahn).
3. Swiss Federal Railways (Schweiserische Bundesbahn).
4. Persons and tons (of goods).
5. Excluding debt interest payments.
Source: W. Puwein, "Die ÖBB-Reform 1992", *op. cit..*

third higher than in Austria (calculated on the basis of purchasing power parities) the Swiss make twice as much use of their railways as the Austrians.

Family benefits

By long tradition, Austria has a well-developed and generous system of family support. It consists of income-tax credits; contribution-free social security coverage for dependents, compulsory education free of charge and monthly cash benefits.[62] Taken together, these measures amounted to some 10 per cent of national income in 1990. The monthly cash benefits are paid out of a central government fund financed by employers' contributions and earmarked shares of general tax revenues. In addition to nationally-administered benefits, the states grant further child benefits (subject to income ceilings). The average benefit per child amounted to some Sch 80 000 per annum with a tendency to rise. From mid-1991, paid parental leave was extended from one to two years for children born after June 1990 and at the beginning of 1993 tax concessions to families were further increased by a total of Sch 7 billion. By international comparison the amount of family subsidies in Austria is very high. Indeed, together with Belgium and France it is the highest among OECD countries (Table 25).

In general, public support to families may have two different aims: to contribute towards covering the costs of raising children and to help low-income earners.[63] In spite of the system's apparent generosity, Austria's birth rate is one of the lowest in the OECD. Moreover, evidence suggests that the risk of poverty rises steeply with family size. Empirical evidence shows that lower-income groups are the main beneficiaries of some cash benefits, but the ultimate effects on income distribution are blurred by the differential impact of the length of

Table 25. **An international comparison of family support**

	Tax subsidies	Family allowance	Child birth allowance	Maternity benefits		Parental leave
	Two children					
	As a per cent of gross earnings of an average production worker in manufacturing			Per cent of last salary	Weeks	Weeks
Austria	**3.7**	**14.2**	**6.2**	**100**	**16**	**24**
Belgium	11.7	13.7	3.4	80	14	6
Denmark	8.4	5.6		90	30	
Finland	7.4	6.6	1.3	80	17	10
France	7.3	7.1	9.8	84	16	36
Germany	9.4	4.4		100	14	18
Ireland	8.3	3.2	2.6	70	14	
Italy	3.5	7.1		80	20	6
Netherlands	0.0	7.3		100	14	6
Norway	7.1	10.2	2.7	100	22	12
Spain	5.0	0.4		75	14	36
Sweden	1.2	8.7		90	7	12
Switzerland	5.1	6.0	0.6-1.6		10	6 to 24
United Kingdom	3.4	5.9	0.7	90	18	

Source: OECD, Tax/Benefit Position of Production Workers, Paris, 1991 and WIFO. "Die Effizienz der österreichischen Familienpolitik", *Monthly Report* 10/1992, Vienna.

schooling on total cash benefits received and the free access to all public education facilities.[64]

The goals of Australian family policy have occasionally been defined in programmatic terms. Official statements refer to the extra financial burden that families with children have to bear and for which family benefits are intended to (partly) compensate. This leaves wide scope for interpretation of the redistributional design of family policy and, indeed, the actual stance of policy has shifted over time. Whereas up to the mid-1950s support was targeted towards low-income families, coverage was extended subsequently and motives of horizontal redistribution gained ground. This was underlined when, in the late 1960s, income ceilings on benefits were waived, giving high income earners greater benefits from existing tax allowances than low-earners. In the 1970s, family subsidies shifted away from tax concessions towards flat-rate cash benefits, according to the principle of ''equal treatment for each child''. However, higher income groups still tended to draw relatively greater benefit as their children attend higher education to a relatively higher degree, entitling them to family subsidies for a longer period.[65] Since the later 1980s the emphasis has shifted back to tax concessions, a stance reinforced in 1992 after a Constitutional Court ruling found tax treatment of families inadequate. While maintaining the previous stance of giving tax credits rather than tax allowances, the government reintroduced a progressive benefit schedule by family size (number of children).

Family benefits are financed via a government fund[66] financed from earmarked taxes and employers' contributions based on the payroll. These rise quasi-automatically with nominal incomes and employment and appear to be tied to revenue aggregates with an above-average income elasticity. By contrast, the number of beneficiaries is declining or at best stagnating due to demographic reasons. This relatively comfortable financial position has led to upward pressure on spending, as reserves in the family benefit fund have accumulated. Thus, the level of benefit has risen substantially in real terms over the last decades and new benefits – e.g. at child birth, free school transport and textbooks – have been introduced to use up surplus funds. Those financial reserves which have not been translated into higher benefits have been transferred – directly or indirectly – to other uses. On balance, however, the earmarking of funds and political pressure has made the system very rigid. The new tax credits, for example, were put ''on top'' of the existing scheme thereby further increasing the already very generous support and adding to budgetary strain.[67]

Social security

Present arrangements of the state pension system also put the federation into a highly unfavourable position to resist higher social security spending. Legislation and administration of social security and insurance is, by the constitution, the responsibility of the federal government, but administration has been delegated to independent institutions (''Versicherungsträger'') which are formally autonomous, but essentially execute federal legislation on health, work-accident and old-age insurance. Altogether, there are 28 social security bodies, each one being responsible for a particular risk and/or a specific category of the work force, as well as by regional criteria with management and control boards delegated by the social partner organisations.

Social security contributions cover more or less total expenditure for health and work accident insurance (except for some government subsidies to farmers), but they cover only about 75 per cent of old-age insurance outlays, the remainder coming from central government transfers.[68] In fact, the federation has taken on a legal obligation to make up for the difference between annual pension outlays and contribution revenues. These transfers currently amount to 7 per cent of central government expenditure. Government subsidies to the pension system tend to rise over time, not only in absolute, but also in relative terms as retirement expenditure outpace contributions. This is partly due to demographic shifts, to early retirement and ''structural'' factors consisting mainly in echo-effects of discretionary benefit increases. Thus, in order to limit the burden on the federal budget the government has occasionally passed on the rising costs to the actively insured by raising contributions. In fact, employees' pension contribution rates have doubled from 11 per cent to almost 23 per cent of gross wages and salaries over the last three-and-a-half decades. They are now one of the highest in the OECD area, due to the combined effects of an elderly population, a low effective retirement age and generous benefits. Moreover, a number of measures have been taken over the last decade to curb the rise in expenditure.

Having committed itself to a financing ''guarantee'' for whatever size the current deficit happens to be, the government has to bear the full incremental costs of the widening gap between expenditure and the contribution base[69]

(Diagram 20). Among the institutional factors contributing to this increasing budget burden, three may be identified:

a) *Split of responsibilities.* As has been pointed out, the social partners play an important role in the formulation and implementation of social policy, representing and controlling the management of the social insurance bodies, and participating in social policy legislation. As a rule, both tasks are carried out by the same people both on the employers and the employees side. As social insurance covers both employers and employees, and both groups are liable to contribution, there is a common interest in increasing benefits while avoiding increases in contribution rates.[70] Thus, all parties concerned tend to invoke the "commitment" of the Bund to pay one-third of total outlays. A recent study undertaken under the auspices of the social partners and dealing with long-term problems of the pension system, sees no scope for alleviating the financial burden of the Bund.[71]

b) *Unclear goals.* The financial share of the Bund in retirement expenditure is often justified by the existence of non-contributory elements in the pension system. Thus, there is a minimum level for pensions even for those whose contributions would give them lower entitlements. Furthermore, certain periods out of work – *e.g.* unemployment, sickness, maternity, schooling, military service – count for pension rights, although the beneficiary pays no contribution. However, the exact amount of these non-contributory elements has rarely been quantified, while the law provides for compensation for some of these items from separate funds (thus, amounts required to cover minimum pensions are paid by the Bund under a separate heading). The costs of benefits involved are thus not very visible to the insurance "customers".

c) *Time lag between political benefits and financial costs.* In some instances, the full costs of a decision to raise benefits become visible only with a long time lag. This is particularly relevant for a retirement scheme where more generous benefits extend with every age cohort and costs increase progressively as the system matures. Also, for a system financed on a "pay-as-you-go" basis a comfortable actual financial position may create an illusion on long-term requirements. Thus, in Austria, a "fiscal dividend" in cyclical boom periods has

Diagram 20. **SHARE OF FEDERAL CONTRIBUTIONS TO THE PENSION SYSTEM**

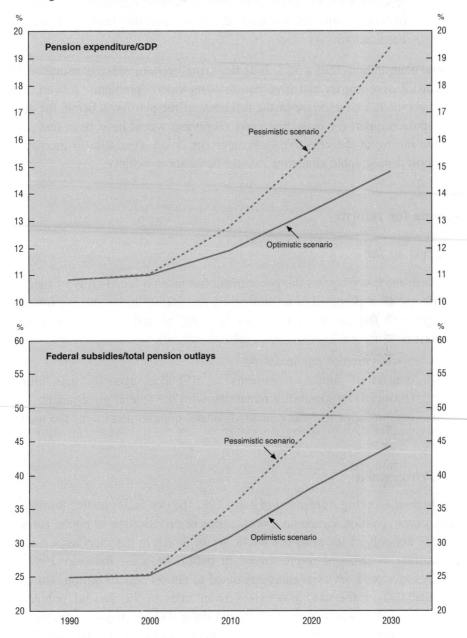

Source: Beirat fuer Wirschafts- und Sozialfragen, Soziale Sicherung im Alter.

77

repeatedly led to increases in pension benefits beyond the regular cost-of-living adjustments with disregard for the long-term financial implications.

Federal contributions thus tend to hide the "true" cost of old-age insurance, blur its redistributive impact and give rise to "free-rider" problems. Indeed, if the active population were aware of the full costs of the pension scheme, the apparent popular support for extending early retirement would have been less strong and the raising of the effective retirement age, a key condition in meeting the long-term demographic challenge, would be easier to achieve.

Agenda for reform

Progress so far

Over the last six years the government has taken a broad array of measures in different areas designed to reform public sector institutions and improve their management. The measures taken so far may be grouped into three broad categories:
- privatisation of public assets;
- transfer of public assignments to off-budget agencies with ultimate (financial) responsibility remaining with the federal government;
- legal reforms to reduce major financial commitments over the medium term.

Privatisation

In their Working Agreement of early 1987 the two major parties forming the government coalition agreed on a programme of privatisation of public assets as a means not only of lowering the public sector deficit in the short term, but also of ensuring a sustained improvement in public finances. Between 1987 and 1989 net receipts from asset sales amounted to almost Sch 20 billion. However, less than half of the total was raised from sales to the general public. For instance, the Mint was sold to the National Bank.[72] Other major "privatisation" measures concerned Austrian Airlines, the major banks and the Austrian Tourist office.

Since 1990 active privatisation has virtually ceased, partly due to stock market weakness. While federal participation in some important companies (such as the national airline and financial institutions) has been allowed to fall below the earlier threshold of 51 per cent (as the state did not participate in the issuance of additional equity to the private market), overall, "privatisation" has resulted in only a small fall in the federal government share in those companies where it has held a stake, from about 75 per cent to 66 per cent. Excluding the special case of the Mint (which was a federal enterprise) the nominal value of state participation fell only by Sch 4½ billion between 1987 and 1990, for which the federal government received earnings of some Sch 11 billion.[73]

Transfers to off-budget agencies

The Working Agreement listed a number of possibilities for moving federal agencies and enterprises off-budget, a process often referred to as corporatisation. The following projects have been carried through: Schönbrunn castle and zoo; waterways agency; federal real estate agency; public debt management agency; the merging of special agencies for road construction and management; and Austrian Federal Railways (ÖBB).

A new law of 1992 provides for the transformation of the ÖBB from a Federal enterprise into a public corporation. By splitting up the Railway organisation into two separate agencies – infrastructure and operation – it is intended, according to the working agreement of the government parties, "to boost productivity and efficiency of railway transportation of people and goods". Moreover, the new structure is in line with EU guidelines providing for a future utilisation of the national railway infrastructure by different customers (international companies) under competitive conditions. Nevertheless, the Minister of Transport retains the powers to:

- issue general rules for ÖBB "in order to enforce transportation policy guideline and even to give specific orders in cases of emergency;
- appoint two-thirds of the members of the supervisory board and exert management control;
- define and commission services in the general public interest. However, these commercially non-viable services will be refunded to the ÖBB by the government in line with rules set by the Ministers of Transport and of Finance.

The government also remains responsible for the maintenance and expansion of the railway infrastructure, for the use of which the ÖBB will pay user fees.

All regulations concerning personnel, pay and retirement remain unchanged, although the new management has to negotiate new regulations with labour representatives which will be applicable to new entrants as from 1995.

Studies on the subject are on balance sceptical about the advantages of extra-budget financing.[74] As a rule, extra-budget financing will constitute only a postponement of budget obligations rather than an actual reduction. In this way, it constitutes an *ex-ante* burden on future budgets adding to budget rigidity and reducing transparency, due to violation of the principles of budgetary unity and comprehensiveness (and contributing to even greater complexity in the fiscal structure). Moreover, insofar as moving programmes off-budget is increasingly used in order to secure financing of public investment, and the debt interest burden will still ultimately fall to the state, the extent to which it is a mere accounting device depends on the financial management reforms undertaken, especially the provision of incentives for securing optimal financing conditions. The example of Deutsche Bundesbahn (DB) shows what can be achieved in the way of productivity improvement, but this result was achieved by a management board recruited from the private sector; an essential precondition for this achievement was the consent of labour representatives and strong backing by the government. Both factors will remain crucial to the success of the ÖBB reform.

Table 26 shows that off-budget financing has anyway been on the rise during the 1980s. Between 1981 and 1990 annual amounts spent almost tripled, to a total of nearly Sch 17 billion. This helped to partly compensate for the decline of on-budget federal investment expenditure as from 1987. The share of total federal investment expenditure financed off-budget rose from one-fifth in the early 1980s to 45 per cent in 1980. Usually, as in the case of the road construction and management agency, the independent entity concerned takes up loans on the capital market to finance the infrastructure building projects, with interest and debt repayments remaining within the federal government budgets. While such arrangements help to alleviate short-term constraints on public investment, the cumulation of debt and annuities set clear limits to this strategy. As can be seen from the table, annual payments due from the federal budget are quickly catching up with the total volume of off-budget financing. Such payments are

Table 26. **Off-budget financing of federal government investment expenditure**

	Off-budget investment		Federal transfers to off-budget agencies
	Sch billion, current prices	Per cent of total federal investment	Sch billion, current prices
1981	6.1	19.0	2.5
1985	12.8	32.2	7.1
1988	14.4	37.7	13.9
1989	15.8	43.1	16.8
1990	16.9	44.7	15.9
1993 (projection)	..	..	19.1
1994 (projection	..	..	19.5
1995 (projection)	..	..	23.6

Source: Fleischmann, Lödl, van der Bellen, *op. cit.*

projected to burden the federal budget by some Sch 24 billion by 1995, a rise by almost 50 per cent within only five years (Table 26).

The Motorway and Transit Road Financing Agency (ASFINAG) provides an illustrative example of the implications of off-budget financing. Founded in 1982 to raise long-term capital for the financing of highway construction and maintenance, its responsibilities were later extended to the financing of railway infrastructure and public administration buildings. Expenditures of the agency are financed by receipts from road toll fees and by federal transfers covering current debt service and repayment costs. During the 1980s the operation of the agency helped to maintain a high level of public investment while lowering the federal budget burden, but the long-term consequences have been less favourable. The agency's own receipts from toll fees have stagnated, while federal transfers have doubled and are set to rise further (Diagram 21). Since the agency, in its operations, incurs administrative costs but is not subject to market constraints and risks, on-budget financing might, from a long-term perspective, even have meant lower budgetary commitments.

Legal reforms

In recent years, the government has taken major initiatives to facilitate structural adjustment in key areas of spending: in 1993, a comprehensive reform of the old-age insurance system took effect; furthermore, a reform bill concerning career and salary patterns in the public sector has been drafted. The major thrust

Diagram 21. **EXPENDITURE AND REVENUES**
OF MOTORWAY FINANCING AGENCY

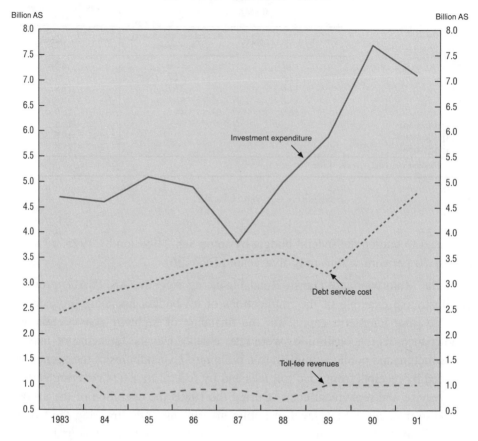

Billion AS

Source: Obermann, Scharmer, Soukup 1993, *op. cit.*

of the pension reform is to improve pension entitlements for parents raising children but also, more fundamentally, to strengthen the ''insurance principle' by bringing individual benefit entitlements closer in line with accumulated contribution payments. The new measures taken will, on balance, increase benefits and are thus not expected to affect federal annual subsidies, but potential cost-saving measures, like the switch to net earnings as the yardstick for the annual cost-of-living adjustment, or the raising of women's retirement age to the level obtaining for men, should produce tangible savings in the long run. On the other hand, the incentives provided by the reform to postpone individual retirement appear too weak to raise the – by international standards – very low retirement age and allow the system to cope with the demographic challenges ahead.

What more needs to be done

The measures taken so far do not appear to go far enough in controlling the growth of budget deficits and in enhancing incentives for efficient and effective government. Other Member governments have moved farther in public sector reform, and understanding of which reforms work and why is improving.[75] Left to evolve in its current financial and organisational framework, the Austrian public sector faces the prospect of gradually deteriorating finances and of relative declines in performance (compared to those of other countries). Given the relative weight of the public sector in the Austrian economy, this is likely to be harmful to the overall development of the economy. A crucial first step in reversing these trends would be to subject the sector as a whole to more binding financial disciplines. These provide the necessary foundation upon which other public sector reforms – for example, in the areas of civil service salaries, corporatisation and systems for monitoring performance – could be laid.

Streamlining fiscal federalism

No major steps have as yet been taken to make the distribution of public revenues among different levels of government less complex and more transparent. A guiding principle for any reforms should be to strengthen the financial accountability of lower government levels. While arguments could be adduced in favour either of greater local autonomy or greater centralisation, it appears that the Austrian system does not fully benefit from either. To be more consistent with the federal nature of the Austrian constitution, the states should be able to rely on their own tax revenues to finance their constitutional responsibilities. Earmarked transfers from the central government, especially costs and expenses defrayed by the federation, should, in this case, be eliminated in favour of own taxes, or at least larger shares of shared taxes. There are limits to the extent to which tax regulations and tax rates may differ by region, particularly in a small country like Austria. However, regional and local governments, often pushed by popular demand, will be inclined to increase spending on ''merit goods'' beyond efficient levels unless they are made financially responsible and accountable for their spending decisions and are fully aware of the full (opportunity) costs involved in each particular case.

As far as local communities are concerned there does not seem to be an urgent need for reform towards more financial autonomy. It seems to be more important to ensure their financial stability. A large step in this direction was made with the tax reform of 1993 which includes complete abolition of Gewerbesteuer (a tax on the profit of industry and trade) and replacement by Kommunalsteuer (an upgraded version of payroll tax). Municipalities will therefore have at their disposal a tax which has a more stable tax base than Gewerbesteuer. The latter's tax base was very negatively affected by the present recession.

In view of Austria's imminent EU membership, initiatives will need to be taken to adjust the federal constitution and, *inter alia*, strengthen legal responsibilities of the states. In this connection, the coalition partners have expressed the intention of reforming the allocation of competences between the Federation and the Länder to take account of the principles of subsidiarity, the need to strengthen direct Länder administration and to reduce indirect federal administration. Indeed, this would appear to be a good occasion to extend reform considerations to aspects of fiscal federalism and, by fostering fiscal responsibilities of states and communities, move towards both higher degree of transparency and efficiency in the management and use of public resources.

Trimming the size of the public sector

Given the still relatively large size of the public sector in Austria, it may be argued that some of the activities presently carried out by public authorities would in fact be best provided by private agencies. There are a number of examples – ranging from manufacturing of medical supplies to chemist's shops to agricultural laboratories – where public ownership or management may have originated accidentally and where reasons for maintaining public sector involvement no longer exist. On a somewhat larger scale, recurrent problems with the nationalised industries suggest that the privatisation programme needs rapidly to be completed. Subsidies to cover past losses will burden the federal budget for many years to come, at an annual amount currently of Sch 5 to 8 billion. This drag on budget flexibility should not be allowed to increase further. The drive for privatisation has stalled in recent years, but the coming recovery should provide the opportunity for future moves in this direction.

Improving the management of public agencies

To the extent that the fiscal system in Austria continues to rely on a corporatist approach, rather than one based on full privatisation, steps need to be taken to improve the co-ordination between central government and the agencies involved. The transformation of the ÖBB from a federal enterprise to a public company is a case in point, intended to strengthen management responsibilities and raise operational productivity. However, taken by itself, such a step is probably not sufficient to ensure better allocation of public resources. Indeed, central government transfers to the ÖBB are set to rise rather than fall over the next few years.[76] In order to ensure that the goals of such reforms be met it will be important to ensure that:

- the sector of non-commercial services undertaken in the "public interest" be closely scrutinised;
- the off-budget entity should not be allowed to claim a monopoly for services in the "public interest";
- services carried out in the predominant interest of states and municipalities should at least partly be financed by them;
- scope for higher fares and user costs be fully exploited.

It is also important to set clear and coherent goals. For example, environmental and other social costs of the railways are generally much lower (per unit of output) than those of motorised road transport. The railways could benefit from this if transportation policy were to internalise the external costs of road transportation. However, present policy is trying to maintain competitiveness of railway transport by subsidising it. In doing so, market prices for transportation services are, on average, reduced, boosting demand beyond optimal levels. Production and distribution of semi-public goods and services – and with them consumption patterns and residential structures – would be less distorted if the implications of socialising costs were more fully recognised and identified. Indeed, in the case of public funds and off-budget agencies, if government subsidies are involved, their purpose and amount should be clearly defined. In particular, unconditional deficit coverage (such as obtains in the Austrian pension fund) should be avoided as it is bound to weaken incentives for expenditure restraint and efficient management.

IV.   Conclusions

Given the deteriorating external environment, the performance of the Austrian economy in 1993, while showing signs of weakness, was rather favourable. Supported by continuing consumption growth, GDP receded only slightly, while the rise in unemployment accelerated moderately, the standardised jobless rate of just over 4 per cent remaining well below the European average. At the same time, consumer price inflation subsided slightly and the current account remained in broad balance.

With slightly positive growth in the second half of the year, the recession has probably bottomed out and should now give way to a gradual recovery of demand. However, insofar as exports are likely to be the main driving force, the pace of expansion will probably be slow in 1994, given the modest outlook for growth in continental Europe. Consumer spending should continue to support activity, but with investment remaining subdued, GDP growth may not return to trend before 1995. In this case, unemployment may keep rising for most of 1994. Insofar as this development could adversely affect confidence, or the expected recovery in export demand be delayed, the outlook is subject to preponderantly negative risks.

The export sector has been the main source of the recession. Austria's most important export markets are those which were either hit hardest by the international recession or where currency realignments seriously undermined the price competitiveness of Austrian suppliers. The slump in foreign demand was felt particularly strongly in tourism and manufacturing industry, with the latter also coming under pressure on domestic markets because of low-price imports of standard goods from neighbouring eastern European countries. What prevented the recessionary forces from abroad from spreading and further depressing activity was the resilience of household demand, notably for services and construction. One of the most remarkable features of developments in 1993 was the resistance of consumer confidence to the adverse trend in the export-oriented sector.

This relatively benign picture may be explained partly by overall employment stability, but may be attributed, also, to the benefits of a credible macroeconomic policy mix. In Austria, this has been composed of three elements: the ability of centrally agreed wage negotiations to produce relatively flexible real wage settlements, giving priority to jobs over pay rises; the monetary commitment to exchange-rate stability based on the "hard currency" option; and fiscal policy consolidation, based on public expenditure restraint, but allowing, in the short-term, the use of automatic stabilisers.

In this recession, as previously, an essential stabilising element has been the combination of social partnership and the centralised wage bargaining system, which tends to promote wage discipline. Thus, in order to ensure wage moderation and decelerating inflation, thereby promoting international competitiveness, the social partners initiated a "stability pact" in the autumn of 1993. In conjunction with the moderate collectively-agreed wage increase for 1994, the effects should be to create the basis for recovery, building on the projected pick up in export demand. Inflation should fall to below 3 per cent and the current account should remain in balance. Nevertheless, having been for many years a leader in price stability, Austria is now expected to have an inflation performance only slightly better than the OECD average. Uniform pay increases, while delivering an above-average degree of real wage flexibility, also tend to give a high weight to inflation in the sheltered sectors, perpetuating inflation inertia in those sectors and generating cost pressures in the exposed sector, undermining competitiveness there and squeezing profits. In this respect, the wage-bargaining system both tends to retard adjustment in the short term and to create certain longer-run structural rigidities and allocational distortions.

Hence, while retaining its evident benefits, there is a need for a reorientation of wages and incomes policy. In particular, the collectively-agreed wage needs to be more geared to productivity trends and price increases in the exposed sector, with the effective wage in individual firms also reflecting more closely the profit situation. Indeed, some progress has already been made in this direction with the "opening clause" agreement attached to the last wage accord which allows some case-by-case wage flexibility. In conjunction with such moves, however, measures should be taken to increase competition in the sheltered sectors, where it appears that profit margins have remained high, with the pass-through from schilling appreciation to domestic prices being rather small. The coming into effect of the European Economic Area in January 1994 has been used as an opportunity for redesigning the domestic regulatory and competition-law framework to produce more effective domestic competition, a process which will be reinforced in the event of entry into the European Union.

At an aggregate level, inflation expectations are anchored by the established credibility of the "hard currency" option: the link to the Deutschemark. Foreign investor confidence in the Austrian currency is now so well entrenched that the country was able to avoid the disruptions caused by the recent strains in the ERM: the currency disturbances of September 1992 and August 1993 generated little or no speculation against the schilling. In fact, short-term interest rates were allowed to fall below German rates in late 1993, indicating an exceptional negative risk premium against the anchor currency. To the extent that policy credibility may owe much to the stabilising process through which wage flexibility prevents an overvaluation of the real exchange rate, while wage expectations are anchored by currency stability, exchange-rate and incomes policies tend to reinforce each other.

In Austria's case, an extensive system of credit subsidies insulates large sectors, most importantly residential construction, from interest-rate disturbances. The problem is that such subsidies have costs, in the form of resource misallocation and cross-subsidisation, which need to be reduced and eventually eliminated. This is all the more important because, despite the – by international standards – traditionally high overall investment ratio, Austria remains prone to "structural" supply side deficiencies. The question arises whether the high level of overall investment is allocatively sound. Indeed, the existence of generous tax subsidies creates a presumption that in many instances tax avoidance may be an overriding investment motive.

It should also be noted that the weakening in the labour market has been accompanied by a secular trend towards higher unemployment among older and longer-term unemployed. Unemployment, although measured at around $4\frac{1}{4}$ per cent of the labour force, is high by past standards. Yet, only a small part of it is cyclical, as is evidenced by its continued increase throughout the boom period and the relatively small extra rise since the beginning of the recession. A substantial part of overall labour slack – which has to some extent been exacerbated by immigration – is cushioned by early retirement. While this keeps the rise in "open" unemployment in check and allows firms to alleviate the payroll burden, it is a costly way for the public sector to deal with the unemployment problem. Making early retirement benefits less generous would help to reduce the implicit incentive to voluntary unemployment, while enhancing the flexibility of labour supply and wage levels.

Budgetary developments have been mixed in recent years. Consolidation proceeded by and large as planned between 1987 and 1991, when the federal deficit was reduced from over 5 per cent to $3^{1}/_{4}$ per cent of GDP; but it stalled in 1992 and, under the impact of the recession, reversed in 1993. Progress made in the earlier years may have created the illusion that – abstracting from the cyclical worsening – deficit reduction is "on track". However, it is not clear that consolidation has yet been brought onto a sustainable basis. Looking at the underlying trend, Federal expenditures continue to outpace revenues, as witnessed by the rising difficulties encountered in annual budget negotiations to contain the deficit – and, indeed, as confirmed by medium-term projections made on assumptions of unchanged tax and expenditure policies.

Furthermore, the thrust of consolidation has gradually shifted away from the expenditure to the revenue side. In some instances, tax hikes in Germany (to cover the costs of reunification) have been seen as an occasion to follow suit without weakening external competitiveness – as, for example, with the mineral oil tax. Likewise, revenue losses expected from the 1994 tax reform are not being accompanied by a *pari passu* lowering of federal expenditure, but are largely "counter-financed" by raising other taxes. This trend conflicts with announced medium-term goals and is worrying. So far, Austria has been able to avoid many of the adverse consequences of an overburdened public sector. Allocative distortions have not seriously constrained GDP growth and the evidence available gives no indications of substantial crowding-out effects. However, generous social transfers have probably reduced labour supply, as labour force participation among older workers is now one of the lowest among OECD countries. Any further increase in fiscal pressure runs the risk of producing undesirable side-effects. Moreover, some future policy commitments are set to put additional claims on government resources, which will have to be accommodated and reconciled with the need for deficit reduction: among those are the envisaged membership of Austria in the European Union and, in the longer term, the ageing of the population.

As recovery from the present recession promises to be slow, there is a risk that decisive budget consolidation could be further delayed. This should not be allowed to happen, as efforts required will only be made greater by postponement and probably more painful. Fiscal consolidation should from now on focus on expenditure cuts and tackle the more underlying institutional impediments in order to make sustainable progress. Indeed, there are a number of mechanisms making for upward pressure on federal spending. Several of them concern financial relations between different public authorities, especially the central, regional and local governments ("fiscal federalism"). The split of responsibilities for spending and financing, associated in important cases, such as state teachers' salaries, with quasi-automatic access to federal budget funds, together with unclearly defined goals and criteria for public financial support, have been identified as the main causes for rising fiscal strain.

While many of the problem areas have been recognised as such by the Austrian authorities, reform measures taken so far have not gone far enough to tackle the problems at their root. Thus, neither the 1993 pension reform nor the 1994 reform of the Federal Railways appear to ensure substantial lasting relief for federal expenditure; and the draft salary reform would even add to spending pressures. Prospective membership of Austria in the EU and its implications should provide a good opportunity for accelerating fiscal reform. This goes also for the Austrian federal structure. Negotiations are currently under way to adjust the Federal Constitution to this new era; this should provide an excellent occasion to extend such considerations to the fiscal aspect – with the goal of giving the provinces a degree of financial autonomy consistent with their spending responsibilities.

Policy measures taken in various areas over recent years show that the government, the Central Bank and the social partners are well aware of the challenges ahead and the course of action required if Austrian economic performance is to remain satisfactory. The benefits to be gained from a consistent and coherent macroeconomic strategy are clearly demonstrated by Austrian monetary policy, where the credibility of the stable exchange rate and anti-inflation commitment, accumulated over many years, has allowed Austria an extra margin of flexibility in lowering policy-controlled interest rates. Measures adopted in the fiscal area have also allowed a relatively flexible response to the recession. However, to retain the required degree of flexibility and consistency requires more decisive and sustained budgetary consolidation as well as action on a range of structural reforms. There is every reason to believe that such reforms, once made, would create the basis for sustainable economic growth.

Notes and references

1. See *Economic Survey of Austria, 1993*, Table 10.

2. In the first nine months of 1993, the number of insolvencies was over 1 500 (with outstanding net losses of Sch 26 billion), one-third higher than one year earlier.

3. Empirical evidence, in fact, suggests that the real interest rate elasticity of business investment is one of the highest among the smaller countries of the OECD. See R. Torres, P. Jarrett, and W. Suyker, "Modelling Business Sector Supply for the smaller OECD countries", OECD, Department of Economics and Statistics *Working Paper 71*, 1989.

4. In the recession of 1981, when output declined by less than $\frac{1}{2}$ per cent, the savings ratio fell by almost $2\frac{1}{2}$ percentage points.

5. See Brandner, P. and P. Mooslechner, "Ökonomische Bedeutung und Problematik der Verschuldung privater Haushalte", WIFO, *Monatsberichte 8/92*.

6. This measure of the unemployment rate is based on the traditional reporting of labour market data, which excludes self-employed. The unemployment rate normally used by the OECD for projections and international comparisons, on the other hand, is based on microcensus data, which includes self-employed and hence gives a lower unemployment rate.

7. See Felix Butschek, *Der osterreichische Arbeitsmarkt – von der Industrialisierung bis zur Gegenwart*, WIFO, Vienna, 1992, for a full historical analysis of the Austrian labour market.

8. At the same time, excessive labour shortages were avoided through the absorption of an initially very large agricultural and craft sector, and by drawing on foreign workers: at its peak in 1973, foreign labour accounted for $8\frac{3}{4}$ per cent of total employment.

9. Between 1960 and 1980 dependent employment grew by some 500 000, of which 200 000 were in the public sector.

10. In 1991, the duration of benefits for maternity leave was increased from one to two years.

11. This was originally intended as compensation for the expected introduction of the European Economic Area in 1993, as under the terms of the EEA agreement, EU and EFTA nationals, accounting for about 1 per cent of the labour force, would no longer require work permits. However, the delay in formation of the EEA meant that this change represented a *de facto* tightening of the restriction.

12. For example, in 1992 workers aged over 50 accounted for 41 per cent of those out of work for more than one year, but only 20 per cent of the total unemployed.

13. Austria moved from a position of sixth lowest (GDP-deflator) inflation-rate country in the OECD in 1990 to eighteenth lowest in 1993.

14. The 1992 increase in the mineral oil tax boosted inflation in that year by an extra $\frac{1}{2}$ point, while higher charges by municipalities continued to take effect in 1993.

15. Insofar as exporters to Austria may have practiced price discrimination (*i.e.* charged higher prices in Austria than elsewhere on equivalent products due to a perceived lower elasticity of demand), this would represent the extent to which the foreign exporter – rather than the domestic importer – "captured" the benefits of exchange rate appreciation. There is some evidence for this type of behaviour; see OECD, *Economic Survey of Austria*, 1989/1990, p. 63.

16. The unexplained weakness of imports, as of exports, could also be tied to difficulties in collection of trade statistics after the abolition of EU border controls as of 1 January 1993.

17. Tourist volumes from Germany fell by 4 per cent; and those from Italy, 22 per cent. Austrians have also participated in these demand shifts, with some substitution of foreign for domestic travel taking place.

18. Participation in the EEA thus required comprehensive legislative changes. The most important reform measures are incorporated in the EEA-Financial Adaptation Act (EWR-Finanzmarktanpassungsgesetz), including, *inter alia*, a reform of the Banking Act (Bankwesengesetz) and legislation on money laundering; the Insurance Act (Versicherungsaufsichtsgesetz); the Stock Exchange Act (Börsegesetz); the Competition Act (Wettbewerbsgesetz); the Product Liability Act (Produkthaftungsgesetz); the Consumer Protection Act (Konsumentenschutzgesetz); the Environmental Compatibility Tests Act (Umweltverträglichkeitsprüfungsgesetz); the Colleges Act (Gesetz über Fachhochschul-Studiengänge); as well as acts on individual liberal professions).

19. There was also the desire to cut the foreign debt service burden of the government. See E. Hochreiter and G. Winckler, "The Advantages of Tying Austria's Hands: The Success of the Hard Currency Strategy", Austrian National Bank *Working Paper* No. 9307, October 1993.

20. *Ibid.* In this way, Austria can be viewed as a "pilot example" of a small country joining the European Monetary Union.

21. In the second week of August 1993 there was a speculative attack on the schilling which lasted only a few hours as it was soon shown to be based on unfounded rumours. During this brief period, the central bank lost Sch 12 billion in foreign currency reserves and the money market rate surged temporarily to 15 per cent.

22. A reversal from long-term lending by Austrian banks to foreign borrowers to net repayments may also have reflected weak exports.

23. Virtually all remaining impediments to international capital flows were removed in November 1991.

24. The supply of money cannot be targeted in this case: it adjusts automatically to fluctuations in demand, via changes in central bank holdings of foreign exchange reserves, at the given exchange and interest rate levels.

25. The Austrian National Bank also decided, at the start of 1993, to enlarge the limit on short-term open market operations, widening its scope for a flexible use of this instrument.

26. The bilateral uncovered short term interest differential can be decomposed as follows:

$$R - R_a = \hat{E}_{+1} + \{CRP + ERP\}$$

where R and R_a respectively denote home and anchor-country short term interest rates; $\hat{E}_{+1}$, the expected rate of depreciation of the home currency against the anchor currency (E = Sch/DM); CRP and ERP, the respective country and exchange risk premia of the home country relative to the anchor country. The hard currency policy, if credible, implies that $\hat{E}_{+1}$ and ERP are zero; hence the interest differential reflects only the country risk premium.

27. Net monthly sales since September 1992 averaged Sch 4 to 5 billion (US$ ½ billion). The share of foreign holdings of federal government debt rose from 15.8 per cent in 1991 to 17.3 per cent in 1992.

28. German unification and liberalisation of capital movements in Austria may explain why Austrian long-term rates were slightly *lower* than Germany's prior to mid-1991.

29. Monetary expansion in Germany has been much higher, despite a more restrictive policy stance and weaker economy, in part due to the distorting effects of a more inverted yield curve, and higher public sector borrowing activity, and the greater burden of exchange market intervention.

30. Subsidised credits to industry and housing can take various forms: preferential interest rates, subsidies on interest and annuity payments, guarantees as well as mixed schemes. In each case, the granting of credit or reduction in the cost of credit is made possible by the public sector's action (that is to say, under "non-market" conditions). See "Subsidised Bank Credits in Austria", *Reports and Summaries* of the Austrian National Bank, 2/1993.

31. Part I (Table 4) shows that in 1993, open sector productivity grew 2½ percentage points faster than total economy productivity, but inflation was almost 4 percentage points lower. Hence, the proposed formula would give a collective wage increase of only about 2½ per cent, while the traditional formula would give 3¾ per cent.

32. This was the result of a ruling by the constitutional court that the existing tax system discriminated against families with children, and was not in itself an element of the tax reform programme.

33. Together with the impact of a 20 per cent VAT rate, this will increase the price of petrol by 60 groschen per litre, expected to add ¼ point to CPI inflation.

34. As a result, pensioners may see their benefits grow by only 2.5 per cent in 1994, which is less than the expected inflation rate of 2.8 per cent.

35. Traditionally, transfers from the federal government covered the deficit of the pension scheme up to a level of 101.5 per cent of total expenditure, less revenues from contributions. This ratio has been gradually reduced over the years, so that as of 1994, only the actual level of the deficit will be covered.

36. By contrast, between 1987 and 1990, the expenditure ratio fell markedly, and the tax ratio also fell.

37. Estimates of potential GDP on which these calculations are based are subject to a wide margin of error. In particular, the strong boom of 1988-91 (average growth rate of 3¾ per

cent) may have caused an overestimate of trend GDP, which could exaggerate the cyclical component of the deficit worsening in subsequent years, in turn overestimating the extent of structural tightness. In other words, the likely errors point to an overly rosy picture of progress in budget consolidation in 1992-94.

38.   In 1992, the special VAT rate on motor cars was replaced by a registration tax based on fuel consumption (Normverbrauchsabgabe); mineral oil taxes were raised while the tax base was widened to include heating oil; and beverage taxation was reformed. In 1993, the rate of taxation on interest income (Kapitalertragssteuer) was increased from 10 to 22 per cent replacing all former income and capital taxes on such financial assets. Also, the base for motor vehicle taxation (separate from the car registration tax) was changed from car volume to motor power, and the tax was now to be levied together with liability insurance premia (rather than stamp taxes as formerly).

39.   There are also sectoral redistributional aspects of tax cuts and tax increases. It is expected that the private services sector will on balance lose from tax reform, but all other sectors are net gainers.

40.   See G. Lehner *et al.*, "Die Zweite Etappe der Steuerreform", WIFO, Vienna, October 1993.

41.   Half of rise in unemployment insurance contributions, *i.e.* 0.35 per cent, is borne by the employer, which raises labour costs by $1/4$ percentage point.

42.   The projections are based on the technical assumption of no change in nominal exchange rates after 2 November 1993.

43.   See *Economic Survey of Austria, 1993*, Chapter III, "International openness and economic performance".

44.   On the other hand, rising US interest rates combined with falling German interest rates imply the risk of downward pressure on the dollar/DM exchange rate. This would offset the risk of upward pressure on the Deutschemark within the EMS, thereby re-establishing the likelihood of a stable effective DM and schilling exchange rate.

45.   See, also, for example, OECD, *Economic Survey of Austria 1992/93*, p. 37.

46.   Total federal expenditure is projected to rise by an annual average of 5.7 per cent between 1992 and 1996, total revenues by only 4.1 per cent per annum. See Bundesministerium für Finanzen, *Budgetprognose und Investitionsprogramm des Bundes 1993-96*, Vienna, 1993.

47.   The Secretariat medium-term baseline scenario shows growth of Austrian real GDP averaging 3 per cent as from 1996 onwards, coupled with moderate productivity growth below 2 per cent, allowing the unemployment rate to decline gradually from $5^{1}/_{2}$ per cent to just under 5 per cent.

48.   See Beirat für Wirtschafts-und Sozialfragen, *Soziale Sicherung im Alter*, Vienna 1991. According to this study, the share of total pension outlays to be covered by federal transfers, currently at 27 per cent, will rise (*ceteris paribus*) to 44 per cent by the year 2030 in an optimistic demographic scenario and to 57 per cent in a pessimistic one.

49.   The Bund may be either wholly responsible for legislative provisions or only for the principal legal guidelines which are then specified in detail and executed on the Länder level.

50.   The states levy only minor taxes like a fire protection tax, while the municipalities levy a municipal payroll tax, a property tax, entertainment tax, beverage and icecream tax.

51. Out of total gross revenue to be shared between the different government levels a number of subsidies and transfers to special funds (like the one for family allowances) are deducted beforehand. The percentages of tax revenues then to be passed on to the provinces and municipalities are negotiated for each tax separately and laid down in a federal law, normally being in force for four years.

52. After deducting 13½ per cent of finance grants for special municipal needs, the Länder distribute the municipalities' shares according to the graded population index.

53. See, e.g. WIFO, *Umverteilung durch öffentliche Haushalte in Österreich*, Vienna, 1987; WIFO, "Die Effizienz der österreichischen Familienpolitik", *Monthly Report* 10/1992; OECD, *Economic Survey of Austria 1991.*

54. Thus, while the number of pupils in general compulsory education declined by an annual average of over 2 per cent between 1980 and 1992, the number of teachers rose by an average 1 per cent per annum. The pupil/teacher ratio which in 1970 had been 22, was only 9.5 in 1992.

55. While revenues earmarked for housing subsidies were previously deducted *a priori* from the total disposable for revenue sharing, the Bund now receives a higher gross revenue share and pays a fixed proportion of 9.22 per cent as transfer to the provinces – basically a change from net to gross budgetary accounting.

56. See OECD, *Economic Survey of Austria, 1991.*

57. Indeed, such a move was envisaged by the Bund at the time, but was rejected by the Länder.

58. Puwein, W. "Reform des ÖBB-Gesetzes", WIFO, *Monthly Report* 3/1992. Nevertheless, such an international comparison should be interpreted with care, bearing in mind national differences in the geographical and legal infrastructure as well as different degrees of policy intervention into business operations.

59. Besides, the competitive situation (low fuel prices, cheap air fares) narrows the scope for increasing train fares.

60. Brunnbauer A., R. Dennerlein, R. Hansen and A. Netzler, *Verteilungseffekte der Verkehr-sausgaben in bezug auf ausgewähle Bevölkerungs-und Einkommensgruppen*, Leitershofen, 1991; and Puwein, W., "Verteilungswirkungen des Verkehrswesens", in WIFO, *Umverteilung durch öffentliche Haushalte in Österreich*, Vienna, 1987.

61. According to calculations made for daily commuters within a range of 25 kilometres, the unit train fare per kilometre is less than half the unit fuel cost for one person in a car (Puwein, 1992). With respect to transport, ÖBB has granted tariff reductions for agricultural and forestry products, construction material, raw materials and basic goods. These exemptions which distort competition have been abolished as they violate EEA regulations.

62. For children up to working age (for students up to the age of 27); lump-sum post-natal payments and payments benefits for subsidised school transport.

63. Some measures are designed to promote education and health policy goals. Thus, textbooks in compulsory education are delivered free of charge. The child birth allowance granted on the condition of certain medical examinations to be passed has reduced infant mortality substantially.

64. WIFO, *Umverteilung durch öffentliche Haushalte in Österreich*, Vienna, 1987.

65. To some extent, though, this effect has been compensated by the disbursement of scholarship to students of modest social background.

66. About 70 per cent of its revenues come from employers' contributions amounting to 4.5 per cent of payroll, the rest mainly from general tax revenues. These tax revenues are transfers under two different headings: one is a 2.29 per cent share of direct taxes ("Steueranteil"), the other a lump sum of Sch 9.5 billion taken at a ratio of 3:1 from wage tax and other income tax.

67. Indeed, it has proved impossible to accommodate the financial effects of the Constitutional Court rulings on higher tax allowances with a moderation of cash benefits in order to keep the overall volume of family support constant.

68. Within the overall 25 per cent or so which the Bund contributes to total pension costs the degree of subsidisation is very different by categories of the work force. Thus, for workers and employees state subsidies cover less than 20 per cent, for self-employed in manufacturing and trade as well as for farmers as much as 70 per cent. For civil servants, who have their own retirement scheme with costs borne on-budget by the territorial authority concerned, implicit subsidisation is even higher as employees contributions cover only about 16 per cent of current retirement benefit outlays.

69. Even when, as a relief measure, insurance contributions are raised, the Bund (but indirectly also provinces and municipalities) still bears part of the burden, via a lower direct tax base, as social insurance contributions are tax deductible.

70. Moreover, it has been argued that there is a common interest of the bureaucracy in different institutions – government, social partners, social security bodies – to expand services and benefits in order to justify given responsibilities and acquire new ones. See C. Smekal, C. Fink, *Wirtschaftspolitische Blätter*, 2/1992.

71. Beirat für Wirtschafts- und Sozialfragen, *Soziale Sicherung im Alter*, Wien 1991.

72. Several regional electricity companies were sold to the federal electricity company ("Verbundgesellschaft") which was, however, subsequently partly privatised itself.

73. Lehner, G., "Der Beitrag der Privatisierung und der außerbudgetären Finanzierung zur Budgetkonsolderung", *Wirtschaftspolitische Blätter* 2/1992, Vienna.

74. Lehner 1992, *op. cit.*; Fleischmann E., M.C. Lödl and A. Van der Bellen, "Außerbudgetäre Finanzierungen", *Handbuch des öffentlichen Haushaltswesens*, M. Gantner (ed.), Vienna, 1991.

75. See OECD, *Public Management Developments: Survey 1993*.

76. However, according to the new legal provisions, such transfers will also include compensation for services rendered.

Annex I

Technical notes

Contributions to price changes (Diagram 6)

The decomposition of the domestic demand deflator is based on the following identities:

$$P_G = GDP/GDPV = (D + E - M)/GDPV = P_D (DV/GDPV) + P_E (EV/GDPV) - P_M (MV/GDPV) \tag{1}$$

$$P_G = (W + Q + T)/GDPV = ULC + UQ + UT \tag{2}$$

where:

GDP	=	gross domestic product
GDPV	=	gross domestic product volume (*i.e.* V denotes volume, as for other variables)
D	=	total domestic demand
E	=	exports of goods and services, N.A. basis
M	=	imports of goods and services, N.A. basis
W	=	total compensation of employees
T	=	net indirect taxes
Q	=	gross non-wage factor income (''profits'') defined as GDP minus (W + T)
ULC	=	W/GDPV
UQ	=	Q/GDPV
UT	=	T/GDPV
P_G	=	GDP deflator
P_D	=	total domestic demand deflator
P_E	=	export deflator
P_M	=	import deflator

Combining equations (1) and (2) above, and taking the differential with respect to time, the following is derived:*

$$\dot{P}_D = U\dot{L}C \frac{(W)}{(D)} + U\dot{Q}\frac{(Q)}{(D)} + U\dot{T}\frac{(T)}{(D)} - \dot{P}_E\frac{E}{D} + \dot{P}_M \frac{M}{D} + R$$

---

* A dot on each variable represents $\dfrac{d_x/d_t}{x}$

99

The various components of per cent changes in the domestic demand deflator are defined as per cent changes in unit labour costs, unit profits, unit tax and terms-of-trade effects, respectively; R indicates effects of compositional changes and equals:

$$R = \frac{(\dot{GDP})}{(D)} \times \frac{(GDPV)}{(DV)} - \frac{E}{D} \times \frac{(\dot{EV})}{(DV)} + \frac{M}{D} \times \frac{(\dot{MV})}{(DV)}$$

Calendar of main economic events

1993

January

The capital gains tax on interest income is raised from 10 to 22 per cent, and converted into a final tax with no further liabilities. At the same time, an amnesty on tax arrears is extended.

The Austrian National Bank lowers the discount rate from 8 to $7\frac{7}{8}$ per cent, while the Lombard rate stays unchanged at $9\frac{1}{4}$ per cent.

February

Austria starts negotiations for EU membership, simultaneously with Sweden and Finland.

The investment tax allowance, for all investment outlays incurred between 1 February 1993 and 31 March 1994, is raised from 20 to 30 per cent. (As of 1 April 1994, it will be lowered to 15 per cent.) Other aspects of the economic stimulus package include an increase in funds available for export credits (Top-Aktion) in 1994 (to Sch 2.2 billion).

The Austrian National Bank lowers policy interest rates simultaneously with the German Bundesbank: the discount rate is reduced from $7\frac{7}{8}$ to $7\frac{1}{2}$ per cent, and the Lombard rate from $9\frac{1}{4}$ to $8\frac{3}{4}$ per cent. The discount and Lombard rates now lie $\frac{1}{2}$ and $\frac{1}{4}$ points, respectively, below their German counterparts.

An export guarantee agreement is reached with the newly independent republics of the former Soviet Union, and soft loans for exports to low per capita income countries are introduced.

March

The Austrian National Bank reduces the discount rate by $\frac{1}{2}$ and Lombard rate by $\frac{1}{4}$ percentage point. Both now lie $\frac{1}{2}$ percentage point below their German counterparts.

A bilateral trade agreement between Austria and Hungary is signed in Vienna. It amplifies on the multilateral trade agreement already reached between EFTA and Hungary.

April

The Austrian National Bank lowers the Lombard rate by $\frac{1}{4}$ point on 23 April, and both the discount and Lombard rates by $\frac{1}{4}$ point on 30 April, to $6\frac{3}{4}$ and 8 per cent, respectively.

May

New wage agreements enter into force. For the various branches of the construction and related industries, collective wage increases range from 4.1 to 4.9 per cent. Workers in the hotel and tourist industry receive an increase in the minimum wage of 3.9 per cent.

The discount and Lombard rates are each reduced by $\frac{1}{4}$ point on 13 May, and by another $\frac{1}{4}$ point on 28 May, to $6\frac{1}{4}$ and $7\frac{1}{2}$ per cent respectively – 1 point below the corresponding German rates (as are the Dutch and Belgian rates).

Austrian Industries reports a loss of Sch 4.8 billion for the year 1992.

June

The government decides on a tax reform for 1994:
- Monthly incomes of up to Sch 11 500 are made tax free, and the general income tax credit is raised from Sch 3 800 to Sch 8 840. Low income earners will be refunded up to 10 per cent of their social security paid-in contributions (negative tax).
- The following taxes on businesses are abolished: wealth tax, professional tax ("Gewerbesteuer") and the special tax on banks. Share dividends and dividend payments of limited partnerships are made subject to a final tax of 22 per cent.
- Small businesses, defined as having yearly turnover of Sch 300 000 (as opposed to 40 000 formerly) obtain relief from the VAT through the "small amounts rule". Businesses with yearly turnover of up to Sch 3 million (hoteliers up to Sch 5 million and small retail traders up to Sch 8 million) qualify for VAT and income taxation at a flat rate.

- To help pay for the estimated Sch 28 billion in tax receipt shortfalls due to the above measures, the corporate tax will be raised from 30 to 34 per cent, and the payroll tax from 2 to 3 per cent, while the tax base for the latter will be widened.

July

A law governing foreigners residing in Austria comes into effect. From now on, yearly quotas on residencies for non-EEA foreign citizens will be established in view of the employment and conjunctural situation. Work permits or longer-residency permits must now be obtained before entering Austria.

An amendment to the general social security law comes into effect:

- Pension entitlements will require at least 25 years of paying into the system, with four years' credit given for time-off for raising children. The basis for calculation of benefits will be the fifteen highest-earning years.
- A job can be held while drawing on a "normal" old-age pension, although above earnings of Sch 7 000 per month, the pension is reduced.
- New types of pensions are introduced: early retirement (as from age 55) due to reduced employability and "sliding pension" (for women as of age 55 and men 60) whereby working time is reduced while partial pensions are drawn (70 per cent of the full pension for a 20 hour week, 50 per cent for a 28 hour week).

The new federal care assistance bill (Bundespflegegeldgesetz) replaces or supplements cash or in-kind assistance for the needy heretofore provided by the Länder. Financing is provided by an increase in social security contributions by 0.4 per cent each for employers and dependent employees, 0.8 per cent for self-employed, and 0.5 per cent for pensioners.

On 2 July, the discount and Lombard rates are reduced by ¼ point each in concert with policy rate reductions in Germany.

Bosnian refugees are now allowed to hold jobs in the private sector, provided that no Austrian nor long-time foreign resident can be found for the job and that the minimum collective wage be respected. The labour market is expected to absorb war refugees through the year 2000.

August

The employment security law, designed to counteract the declining employment prospects for older workers, is introduced. Written justifications to the labour office and compulsory contributions to older-worker retraining programmes may be required in the event of the lay-off of workers over 50, while one-time subsidies are awarded in the event of hiring a worker over 45.

On 15 August, the National Bank counters exchange market speculation against the schilling. As a result, its foreign exchange reserve holdings fall by Sch 11.9 billion, to Sch 132.8 billion. This shortfall is quickly more than made up, however, with the ensuing reflows of foreign currency.

September

A new collective wage agreement is reached for workers in the metal industry. It allows for a 3.8 per cent increase in the collective minimum wage, and a 2.8 per cent increase in the effective wage (however at least Sch 500 and at most Sch 900 per month). Accounting for the lump-sum payment of Sch 2 000 last year, the effective wage increase drops to 2.2 per cent. With the newly-agreed "opening clause", firms in difficulties may avoid giving pay rises if lay-offs can thereby be averted.

On 10 September, following interest rate reductions by the German Bundesbank, the Austrian National Bank lowers the discount rate from 6 to $5^3/4$ per cent, and the Lombard rate from $7^1/4$ per cent to $6^3/4$ per cent.

The governing board of the state oil company ÖMV estimates a 1993 loss of Sch 4.7 billion. A restructuring package envisages plant shutdowns and a reduction in force of 1 200 to 1 500 workers from 12 000 presently, and the adaptation of currently above-average wages and salaries to the chemical industry average.

October

Parliament passes the 1994 Budget, which provides for a federal government deficit of Sch 79 billion (3.6 per cent of GDP).

The packaging law comes into effect. It requires the recycling of packaging all along the distribution chain, with specific quotas to be reached in a step-wise plan by the year 2000.

The federal, state and local governments unite with the social partners on a "Solidarity Pact" of measures to revive the economy and to assure price stability.

The Austrian National Bank lowers the discount rate from $5^3/4$ to $5^1/4$ per cent, and the Lombard rate from $6^3/4$ to $6^1/4$ per cent, in parallel with interest rate reductions by the Bundesbank.

November

The amendment to the Cartel Law introduces a limit on mergers, in view of the approach to EU membership.

1994

January

The new Bank Law enters into force, which takes into account the requirements of the European Economic Area (EEA).

The 1994 tax reform comes into effect.

The earnings of public sector workers are increased by 2.55 per cent (2.5 per cent for railway employees).

February

Following a move by the Bundesbank, the Austrian National Bank lowers the discount rate from $5\frac{1}{4}$ to 5 per cent and the Lombard rate from $6\frac{1}{4}$ per cent to 6 per cent.

STATISTICAL AND STRUCTURAL ANNEX

Table A. Gross domestic product

Sch billion

	Current prices					1983 prices				
	1988	1989	1990	1991	1992	1988	1989	1990	1991	1992
Expenditure										
Private consumption	880.5	935.3	1 000.9	1 059.4	1 127.3	773.0	799.8	830.1	849.8	868.3
Public consumption	288.4	302.9	319.9	348.1	371.8	237.4	239.2	242.1	248.5	253.7
Gross domestic fixed capital formation	371.2	405.8	442.3	482.3	500.5	327.7	347.7	367.7	385.9	390.2
Construction[1]	211.2	229.1	250.6	277.6	299.1	186.4	195.0	206.5	218.3	227.8
Machinery and equipment[1]	159.9	176.7	191.6	204.7	201.4	141.3	152.8	161.2	167.6	162.4
Change of stocks, incl. statistical errors	17.6	12.8	12.9	7.8	2.9	16.5	10.6	20.3	24.1	26.5
Exports of goods and services	587.5	664.3	724.3	789.7	805.6	553.7	610.6	659.9	714.3	716.6
less: Imports of goods and services	578.6	649.4	702.0	772.5	779.6	572.9	621.8	670.4	729.8	739.7
Gross domestic product at market prices	1 566.6	1 671.5	1 798.4	1 914.7	2 028.5	1 335.4	1 386.3	1 449.7	1 492.9	1 515.6
Origin by sector										
Agriculture, forestry and fishing	49.1	52.3	56.7	53.0	50.1	46.5	46.1	48.1	45.6	44.2
Manufacturing and mining	415.7	437.7	475.9	502.3	525.9	376.2	390.9	412.1	421.9	423.9
Construction	105.3	113.5	125.6	140.3	153.6	92.0	96.0	100.7	105.7	120.4
Other	996.4	1 068.1	1 140.2	1 219.2	1 298.9	820.7	853.2	888.8	919.7	927.1

	Current prices					Current prices, percentage distribution				
	1988	1989	1990	1991	1992	1988	1989	1990	1991	1992
Distribution of net national income										
Compensation of employees	821.9	874.4	940.1	1 019.8	1 088.1	71.5	71.4	70.9	72.4	72.8
Net income from property and entrepreneurship and savings of corporations	349.9	373.3	416.3	427.6	443.5	30.5	30.5	31.4	30.4	29.7
Direct taxes on corporations	27.4	33.3	35.6	40.3	48.0	2.4	2.7	2.7	2.9	3.2
Government income from property and entrepreneurship	30.7	33.3	38.1	41.2	45.1	2.7	2.7	2.9	2.9	3.0
less: Interest on public debt and consumer debt	81.0	89.1	103.3	120.7	130.0	7.0	7.3	7.8	8.6	8.7
Net national income	1 149.0	1 225.2	1 326.7	1 408.2	1 494.7	100.0	100.0	100.0	100.0	100.0

1. Excluding V.A.T.

Source: Österreichisches Statistisches Zentralamt, and Österreichisches Institut für Wirtschaftsforschung.

Table B. **General government income and expenditure**

Sch billion

	1984	1985	1986	1987	1988	1989	1990	1991	1992
Operating surplus and property income receivable	23.1	26.2	25.9	29.4	30.7	33.3	38.1	40.8	44.5
Casualty insurance claims receivable	0.2	0.2	0.3	0.3	0.3	0.4	0.4	0.4	0.4
Indirect taxes	216.1	225.9	234.0	245.2	254.9	271.4	287.9	305.8	325.1
Direct taxes	173.7	193.7	203.8	203.3	214.5	214.4	239.0	267.1	296.3
Compulsory fees, fines and penalties	4.1	3.8	3.9	3.9	4.1	4.4	4.9	5.1	5.1
Social security contributions	155.5	167.8	176.0	183.3	191.8	204.3	220.6	238.9	262.2
Unfunded employee welfare contributions imputed	32.8	35.3	37.6	39.6	41.1	43.4	46.0	49.8	53.0
Current transfers n.e.c. received from the rest of the world	0.6	0.7	0.7	0.7	0.6	0.6	0.7	0.9	0.8
Current receipts	606.1	653.6	682.2	705.7	738.0	772.2	837.6	908.8	987.4
Final consumption expenditure	237.8	255.0	270.7	280.4	288.4	302.9	319.9	349.6	375.0
Property income payable	43.1	47.8	51.9	58.4	61.8	66.4	73.1	82.0	87.6
Net casualty insurance premiums payable	0.2	0.2	0.3	0.3	0.3	0.4	0.4	0.4	0.4
Subsidies	35.9	39.2	46.0	47.4	45.1	45.1	47.9	56.4	61.4
Social security benefits and social assistance grants	130.8	142.3	151.1	161.5	167.8	176.4	188.7	199.9	213.2
Current transfers to private non-profit institutions serving household	72.3	76.3	80.4	87.0	85.2	86.4	94.1	103.7	115.4
Unfunded employee welfare benefits	52.3	56.2	59.9	63.4	66.0	70.1	74.5	80.8	85.9
Current transfers n.e.c. paid to the rest of the world	3.5	3.6	3.8	3.9	4.3	4.7	5.5	6.5	6.8
Current disbursements	575.9	620.6	664.1	702.3	718.9	752.4	804.1	879.3	945.7
Saving	30.2	33.0	18.1	3.4	19.1	19.8	33.5	29.5	41.7
Consumption of fixed capital	10.1	10.7	11.3	11.6	11.8	12.2	12.8	13.5	13.8
Capital transfers received net, from:	-25.2	-27.1	-27.5	-26.8	-27.3	-23.1	-27.0	-26.5	-29.9
Other resident sectors	-25.2	-27.1	-27.5	-26.8	-27.3	-23.0	-26.9	-26.3	-29.7
The rest of the world	0.0	0.0	0.0	0.0		-0.1	-0.1	-0.2	-0.2
Finance of gross accumulation	15.1	16.6	1.9	-11.8	3.6	8.9	19.3	16.5	25.6
Gross capital formation	46.3	48.0	52.1	50.7	50.7	55.2	57.3	62.6	66.0
Purchases of land, net	1.7	1.8	2.2	0.7	0.6	0.6	0.7	0.9	0.8
Net lending	-32.9	-33.2	-52.4	-63.2	-47.7	-46.9	-38.7	-47.0	-41.2

Source: Bundesministerium für Finanzen.

Table C. **Output, employment and productivity in industry**

	1982	1983	1984	1985	1986	1987	1988	1989	1990	1991	1992
Output in industry, 1985 = 100 (adjusted for working days)											
Total industry	90.0	90.9	95.6	100.0	101.1	102.1	106.6	112.9	121.6	123.6	122.4
Investment goods	88.5	86.7	89.0	99.9	103.4	95.5	101.1	107.4	127.1	133.5	128.6
Consumer goods	91.7	92.4	97.4	99.9	100.6	99.0	99.0	105.2	109.5	111.6	109.9
Employment, thousands[1]	589.0	565.1	561.4	562.4	558.8	543.6	532.6	536.3	544.8	538.9	520.5
Wages and productivity											
Gross hourly earnings for wage earners (Sch)	82.8	86.8	90.0	95.1	99.3	104.3	107.8	112.6	120.7	127.9	135.3
Gross monthly earnings, employees (Sch)	16 868.7	17 739.9	18 625.9	19 755.4	20 713.3	21 504.5	22 338.9	23 389.5	25 143.5	26 592.8	28 207.7
Output per hour (1970 = 100)	205.9	204.9	203.5	206.7	213.6	216.3	206.7	206.0	208.2	213.0	..
Wages and salaries per unit of output (1970 = 100)	186.6	198.6	208.2	217.6	225.6	236.2	256.0	271.4	290.6	305.0	..

1. Including administrative personnel.
Source: Österreichisches Institut für Wirtschaftsforschung, and Österreichisches Statistisches Zentralamt.

Table D. **Retail sales and prices**

(1985 = 100)

	1982	1983	1984	1985	1986	1987	1988	1989	1990	1991	1992
Retail sales	87.9	94.7	95.5	100.0	101	103.6	108.8	114.0	121.9	131.1	136.0
of which: durables	84.1	97.8	90.5	100.0	108	113.0	125.1	134.5	144.9	156.5	163.1
Prices											
Consumer prices											
Total	88.7	91.7	96.9	100.0	102	103.1	105.1	107.8	111.3	115.0	119.7
Food	90.3	92.6	97.8	100.0	102	103.2	103.9	105.2	108.4	112.8	117.2
Rent	81.2	88.8	95.0	100.0	103	105.6	108.1	111.3	115.9	121.6	128.6
Other goods and services	89.1	91.6	96.7	100.0	101	103.3	105.6	108.7	112.2	115.5	119.9
Wholesale prices											
Total	93.4	94.0	97.5	100.0	95	92.8	92.6	94.3	97.0	97.8	97.6
Agricultural goods	94.4	94.2	98.0	100.0	91	94.5	93.3	93.2	100.1	101.7	91.4
Food	89.3	91.6	96.7	100.0	100	97.4	96.6	96.0	95.2	97.6	102.6
Cost of construction (residential)	91.6	94.9	98.3	100.0	102	105.4	108.8	112.7	117.3	124.2	129.8

Source: Österreichisches Statistisches Zentralamt, and Österreichisches Institut für Wirtschaftsforschung.

Table E. Money and banking[1]
End of period
Sch billion

	1983	1984	1985	1986	1987	1988	1989	1990	1991	1992
Interest rates (per cent)										
Discount rate	3.75	4.50	4.00	4.00	3.00	4.00	6.50	6.50	8.00	8.00
Average bond yield[2]	8.15	7.98	7.74	7.30	6.86	6.58	7.06	8.72	8.69	8.39
Money circulation and external reserves										
Notes and coins in circulation	92.3	93.7	94.5	98.1	102.9	108.4	117.8	124.7	133.4	..
Sight liabilities of the Central Bank	46.9	48.8	46.6	53.0	43.6	39.6	51.1	44.3	38.8	48.9
Gross external reserves of the Central Bank	114.2	118.6	110.5	115.0	114.9	123.4	132.8	130.3	140.1	167.4
of which: Gold	39.4	39.4	39.4	39.5	39.5	39.5	38.6	38.1	37.4	37.2
Credit institutions										
Credits to domestic non-banks	1 000.9	1 114.4	1 211.6	1 333.6	1 438.2	1 579.4	1 688.4	1 846.2	1 994.2	2 129.8
Deposits from domestic non-banks	928.3	989.4	1 058.2	1 170.7	1 259.2	1 312.3	1 404.3	1 503.8	1 613.9	1 680.3
Sight	97.8	102.7	107.5	113.5	129.1	142.2	146.5	155.9	170.8	180.9
Time[3]	109.9	113.9	124.1	162.8	176.3	174.4	198.8	185.8	172.4	136.9
Savings	720.6	772.8	826.6	894.4	953.7	995.7	1 059.0	1 162.1	1 270.7	1 362.5
Holdings of domestic Treasury bills	45.1	46.2	41.0	41.0	51.2	46.9	44.9	53.7	60.4	56.3
Holdings of other domestic securities	224.2	228.2	233.1	249.9	287.0	319.5	345.7	356.1	365.0	342.4
Foreign assets	542.6	633.5	695.9	737.6	751.7	816.9	842.0	843.9	846.8	915.9
Foreign liabilities	559.5	676.7	724.6	772.4	794.7	883.8	933.0	937.8	962.0	1 048.7

1. Totals may not add due to rounding.
2. Average effective yields on circulating issues.
3. Including funded borrowing of banks.
Source: Österreichische Nationalbank, and Österreichische Länderbank.

Table F. The federal budget

National accounts basis
Sch billion

	Outturn								
	1984	1985	1986	1987	1988	1989	1990	1991	1992
1. Current revenue	306.1	330.3	343.7	354.8	389.2	404.6	437.5	473.2	520.0
Direct taxes of households	92.0	102.1	107.6	105.1	129.9	124.8	140.1	154.1	168.1
Indirect taxes	151.5	157.9	164.0	173.1	178.8	190.1	201.2	213.2	229.2
Corporate taxes	17.6	20.2	20.4	19.9	21.0	25.1	26.3	30.5	37.8
Income from property and entrepreneurship	16.7	18.9	18.8	22.4	23.1	24.9	27.6	29.1	33.5
Current transfers from abroad	0.3	0.4	0.3	0.3	0.3	0.2	0.3	0.4	0.2
Other	28.0	30.8	32.6	34.0	36.1	39.5	42.0	45.9	51.2
2. Current expenditure	316.4	340.5	367.5	392.2	403.6	414.7	441.3	488.9	525.6
Goods and services	89.2	95.6	101.2	102.0	104.3	109.0	113.7	122.8	129.5
Subsidies	27.8	30.0	36.4	37.5	34.7	34.1	35.2	42.9	45.5
Public debt	33.8	38.4	42.7	49.4	53.1	58.0	64.3	73.1	78.7
Transfers to abroad	1.0	1.0	1.0	1.0	1.1	1.2	1.6	2.0	2.1
Transfers to public authorities	76.8	82.0	87.6	96.3	105.5	105.5	111.0	121.4	130.7
Transfers to private households	55.7	59.3	62.3	67.6	65.0	64.5	70.5	77.5	86.9
Other	32.1	34.2	36.3	38.4	39.9	42.4	45.0	49.2	52.2
3. Net public savings (1 – 2)	-10.3	-10.2	-23.8	-37.4	-14.4	-10.1	-3.8	-15.8	-5.6
4. Depreciation	2.3	2.4	2.6	2.6	2.7	2.8	2.9	3.1	3.1
5. Gross savings (3 + 4)	-8.0	-7.8	-21.2	-34.8	-11.7	-7.3	-0.9	-12.7	-2.5
6. Gross asset formation	18.0	17.8	18.5	15.5	15.2	15.4	16.0	16.8	15.2
7. Balance of income-effective transactions (5 – 6)	-26.0	-25.6	-39.7	-50.3	-26.9	-22.7	-16.9	-29.5	-17.7
8. Capital transfers (net)	22.6	23.7	24.4	23.2	39.0	34.8	37.8	40.0	40.9
9. Financial balance (7 – 8)	-48.6	-49.3	-64.1	-73.5	-65.9	-57.5	-54.7	-69.5	-58.6

Source: Österreichisches Statistisches Zentralamt.

Table G. **Balance of payments**

Sch million

	1983	1984	1985	1986	1987	1988	1989	1990	1991	1992
Trade balance[1]	-70 753	-76 784	-67 669	-62 231	-65 697	-70 368	-81 727	-90 168	-112 869	-106 365
Exports	278 181	324 606	366 544	342 659	342 714	375 541	427 511	466 065	479 029	487 558
Imports	348 934	401 390	434 213	404 890	408 411	445 909	509 238	556 233	591 898	593 923
Services, net	40 434	48 429	49 085	42 007	40 354	45 062	57 750	73 148	77 546	85 900
Foreign travel, net	42 334	48 529	48 853	44 884	41 349	46 726	58 881	64 666	74 842	67 400
Receipts	94 386	101 026	105 186	106 195	112 030	124 617	141 782	152 441	161 178	159 640
Expenditure	52 052	52 497	56 333	61 311	70 681	77 891	82 901	87 775	86 336	92 240
Investment income, net	-6 696	-7 030	-5 334	-10 104	-10 856	-11 279	-12 324	-10 976	-17 562	-13 083
Other services, net	4 796	6 930	5 566	7 227	9 861	9 615	11 193	19 458	20 266	19 964
Unclassified goods and services	35 777	25 625	18 045	24 631	23 633	21 833	27 841	30 681	36 349	30 456
Transfers, net	-1 456	-1 206	-1 947	-657	-1 023	-433	-1 681	-26	-206	-11 619
Public	-792	-766	-799	-690	-898	-894	-945	-2 138	-2 307	-5 382
Private	-664	-440	-1 148	33	-125	461	-736	2 112	2 101	-6 237
Current balance	4 002	-3 936	-2 486	3 750	-2 733	-3 906	2 183	13 635	820	-1 628
Long-term capital, net[2]	-24 052	-7 096	-3 650	9 928	23 040	6 068	4 450	-10 207	-24 383	7 871
Basic balance	-20 050	-11 032	-6 136	13 678	20 307	2 162	6 633	3 428	-23 563	6 243
Short-term capital, net	19 180	14 740	-6 687	6 719	-18 382	7 082	5 165	8 942	24 818	13 182
Errors and omissions	-6 974	-2 080	11 626	-11 944	2 818	-3 161	-232	-12 967	7 955	8 348
Balance on official settlements[3]	-7 844	1 628	-1 197	8 453	4 743	6 083	11 566	-597	9 210	27 773
Memorandum items:										
Changes in reserves arising from allocation of SDRs, monetization of gold and revaluation of reserve currencies	6 519	4 706	-9 601	-6 960	-4 834	3 266	-2 736	-3 083	1 144	2 184
Allocation of SDRs	0	0	0	0	0	0	0	0	0	0
Change in total reserves	-1 326	6 334	-10 802	1 491	-92	9 351	8 830	-3 723	10 307	29 957
Conversion factor (Sch per dollar)	17.97	20.01	20.69	15.27	12.64	12.34	13.23	11.37	11.67	10.99

1. Including non monetary gold and adjustments to trade according to foreign trade statistics.
2. Including Central Bank.
3. Excluding allocation of SDRs, monetization of gold and revaluation of reserve currencies.
Source: Österreichische Nationalbank.

Table H. Merchandise trade by commodity group and area

Sch billion

	Imports					Exports				
	1988	1989	1990	1991	1992	1988	1989	1990	1991	1992
Total	451.5	514.9	558.1	593.0	594.7	383.5	429.6	467.7	480.0	488.0
By commodity group										
Food, drink, tobacco	24.5	26.8	27.7	29.5	29.1	12.9	15.2	15.2	15.2	15.9
Raw materials	24.6	27.8	25.3	25.4	24.6	20.6	23.4	24.4	21.5	19.9
Mineral fuels, energy	25.4	29.3	35.4	35.5	30.5	4.9	5.5	4.7	4.4	5.2
Chemicals	47.5	52.1	55.3	57.7	58.4	37.2	39.8	39.5	42.8	42.1
Machinery and transport equipment	165.9	191.2	211.6	232.1	234.8	131.0	148.0	175.6	184.0	189.7
Other	163.7	187.6	202.9	212.9	217.3	176.8	197.7	208.3	212.1	215.2
By area										
OECD countries	385.7	437.6	473.6	500.7	502.4	317.2	355.2	383.0	389.4	393.2
EC countries	309.6	351.6	383.0	402.0	403.9	250.3	279.8	304.8	316.2	322.6
Germany	203.0	226.8	245.5	255.0	255.2	139.9	153.9	175.1	187.5	194.5
Italy	40.3	46.2	50.5	52.4	51.3	39.9	45.3	45.8	45.0	42.9
France	17.8	22.7	23.4	25.8	26.3	17.7	20.0	22.2	20.9	21.4
United Kingdom	11.2	12.9	14.4	16.0	16.2	18.1	19.3	18.1	17.4	17.5
EFTA countries[1]	33.2	36.6	39.4	40.8	40.6	41.2	45.6	47.3	44.1	42.2
Switzerland	19.9	21.3	23.8	24.8	23.8	27.6	31.1	32.4	30.6	29.0
United States	15.3	18.6	20.2	23.4	23.5	13.5	15.0	15.0	13.6	12.9
Other OECD countries	27.5	30.7	31.0	34.6	34.3	12.1	14.8	15.9	15.4	15.5
Non-OECD countries										
Eastern Europe[2]	26.7	28.9	31.8	35.7	38.7	29.3	33.1	36.5	43.0	47.3
Africa[3]	7.6	11.5	13.8	12.9	11.0	7.2	7.5	7.5	7.7	6.4
Latin America[3]	5.9	6.5	5.6	6.0	5.4	2.6	2.9	3.1	3.6	4.1
OPEC	7.2	9.4	12.0	12.5	11.5	11.4	11.3	12.8	13.8	13.8
Far and Middle East[3]	20.7	23.9	26.5	31.5	32.2	18.4	20.8	24.2	25.8	26.9
Index, in real terms (1988 = 100)	100	111	123	124	130	100	113	126	133	139
Index of average value (1988 = 100)	100	103	100	100	99	100	98	97	94	92

1. Including Finland.
2. Excluding ex-Yugoslavia.
3. Including countries belonging to OPEC.
Source: Österreichisches Institut für Wirtschaftsforschung.

Table I. Labour-market indicators

	Peak	Trough	1986	1987	1988	1989	1990	1991	1992
					A. EVOLUTION				
Unemployment rate (surveys)									
Total	1983 = 4.1	1973 = 1.1	3.1	3.8	3.6	3.1	3.2	3.5	3.6
Male	1984 = 3.9	1973 = 0.7	3.2	3.6	3.3	2.8	3.0	3.4	3.5
Women	1983 = 5.1	1973 = 1.7	3.1	4.1	4.0	3.6	3.6	3.7	3.8
Unemployment rate (registered)									
Total	1987 = 5.6	1973 = 1.6	5.2	5.6	5.4	5.0	5.4	5.8	5.9
Male			5.1	5.5	5.1	4.6	4.9	5.3	..
Women			5.3	5.7	5.6	5.5	6.0	6.5	..
Youth			2.8	2.7	2.8	2.4	2.6	2.6	..
Share of long-term unemployment			12.6	15.0	12.7	16.7	15.8	19.2	..
Productivity index, 1991 = 100			89.5	90.5	93.8	96.5	98.8	100.0	99.5
Monthly hours of work in industry (wage earners)									
billions of hours			142.1	139.9	141.0	139.9	139.5	138.2	138.2
			B. STRUCTURAL OR INSTITUTIONAL CHARACTERISTICS						
Participation rates[1]									
Global			66.3	67.0	66.9	67.1	67.7	68.4	69.4
Male			81.3	81.2	80.3	80.0	80.1	80.5	80.7
Women			51.7	53.0	53.7	54.3	55.4	56.3	58.0
Employment/population between 16 and 64 years[1]			64.2	64.4	64.5	65.0	65.5	66.0	66.9
Employment by sector									
Agriculture – per cent of total			8.7	8.7	8.2	7.9	7.9	7.4	7.1
– per cent change			-2.4	0.4	-5.4	-1.6	1.2	-4.3	-2.4
Industry – per cent of total			37.8	37.7	37.4	37.0	36.8	36.9	35.6
– per cent change			0.6	0.2	-0.4	-0.2	1.6	2.1	-1.7
Services – per cent of total			53.6	53.7	54.4	55.1	55.3	55.7	57.4
– per cent change			2.7	0.8	1.7	2.3	2.5	2.4	5.1
of which: Government – per cent of total			20.7	21.2	..	..	..	..	..
– per cent change			3.0	3.1	..	..	..	..	..
Voluntary part-time work			7.2	8.0	8.2	9.7	9.9	9.8	..
Social insurance as a per cent of compensation			18.2	18.3	18.5	18.5	18.4	18.1	..

1. Including the self-employed.
Source: Statistisches Handbuch – Österreichisches Institut für Wirtschaftsforschung – OECD estimates – OECD, *Labour Force Statistics.*

Table J. **Public sector**

	1970	1980	1990	1991	1992
	BUDGET INDICATORS: GENERAL GOVERNMENT ACCOUNTS (% GDP)				
Current receipts	39.7	46.4	46.6	47.5	48.7
Non-interest expenditure	37.4	45.6	44.7	45.7	46.4
Primary budget balance	2.3	0.8	1.9	1.8	2.3
Gross interest	1.1	2.5	4.1	4.3	4.3
General government budget balance	1.2	−1.7	−2.2	−2.5	−2.0
of which:					
Federal government	0.2	−2.6	−3.2	−3.6	..
	THE STRUCTURE OF EXPENDITURE (% GDP)				
Government expenditure					
Transfers	4.0	5.9	5.6	5.8	6.0
Subsidies	1.7	3.0	2.7	2.9	3.0
General expenditure	14.7	18.0	17.8	18.2	18.5
Education	2.9	3.9	4.0	..	..
Health	3.2	4.4	4.6	..	..
Social security and welfare	2.6	3.3	3.3	..	..

	TAX RATES	
	Prior to Tax Reform of 1989	Under the Tax Reform of 1989
Personal income tax		
Top rate	62	50
Lower rate	21	10
Average tax rate	12.7	11.5
Social security tax rate[1]		
Blue-collar workers	38.6	38.6
White-collar workers	34.5	34.5
Basic VAT rate	20	20
Corporation tax rate		
Top rate	55	30
Lower rate	30	30

1. The sum of employees' and employers' contributions to health, accident, pension and unemployment insurance.
Source: OECD, *National Accounts;* Ministry of finance.

117

Table K. Production structure and performance indicators

A. Production structure (1985 prices)

	GDP share (per cent of total)					Employment share (per cent of total)				
	1980	1988	1989	1990	1991	1980	1988	1989	1990	1991
Tradeables										
Agriculture	4.2	4.0	3.8	3.8	3.5	1.7	1.3	1.3	1.2	1.2
Mining and quarrying	0.7	0.5	0.4	0.4	0.4	0.6	0.4	0.4	0.4	0.3
Manufacturing	33.5	33.2	33.2	33.2	33.0	40.5	36.8	36.4	36.0	35.3
Non-tradeables										
Electricity	3.7	3.5	3.7	3.5	3.5	1.7	1.8	1.7	1.7	1.6
Construction	10.0	8.0	8.0	8.0	8.1	11.2	9.9	9.9	10.0	10.2
Wholesale and retail trade, restaurants and hotels	19.5	20.0	19.9	20.4	20.6	21.4	23.6	23.9	24.2	24.5
Transport, storage and communication	6.8	7.3	7.5	7.5	7.7	9.6	10.3	10.2	10.2	10.2
Finance, insurance, real estate and business services	17.5	18.7	18.7	18.5	18.7	8.4	9.7	9.9	10.1	10.3
Community, social and personal services	4.2	4.7	4.7	4.7	4.7	5.1	6.3	6.3	6.3	6.4

B. Industrial sector performance

	Productivity growth (sector GDP/sector employment)					Investment share, current prices (per cent of total)				
	1980	1988	1989	1990	1991	1980	1988	1989	1990	1991
Tradeables										
Agriculture	8.6	6.2	0.7	4.2	4.6	6.4	4.8	..	..	..
Mining and quarrying	2.4	2.6	-2.5	9.4	0.9	0.4	0.3	..	..	..
Manufacturing	2.1	9.4	3.5	4.1	2.6	20.5	19.2	..	..	..
Non-tradeables										
Electricity	5.8	-7.2	10.4	-0.0	4.2	6.9	5.1	..	..	..
Construction	0.0	1.4	2.5	1.2	1.1	2.8	2.4	..	..	..
Wholesale and retail trade, restaurants and hotels	0.0	2.8	0.8	3.9	0.9	..	..	..	..	..
Transport, storage and communication	4.9	3.3	5.0	3.5	3.2	..	..	..	..	..
Finance, insurance, real estate and business services	3.2	-0.1	1.2	-0.6	0.1	..	..	..	..	..
Community, social and personal services	1.3	5.1	1.9	1.8	0.3	..	..	..	..	..

Table K. **Production structure and performance indicators** *(cont'd)*

	Numbers of enterprises (per cent of total)					Numbers of employees (per cent of total)				
	1980	1988	1989	1990	1991	1980	1988	1989	1990	1991
C. Other indicators										
Enterprises ranged by size of employees										
1 to 4	18.3	40.3	40.4	38.4	37.7	0.3	0.7	0.7	0.7	0.7
5 to 49	49.0	38.0	37.7	38.6	38.8	11.2	12.5	12.4	12.2	12.4
50 to 499	29.6	19.8	20.0	20.9	21.5	46.6	48.6	48.9	49.8	51.6
more than 500	3.1	1.9	2.0	2.1	2.0	41.9	38.1	38.0	37.3	35.4

	1982	1983	1984	1985	1986	1987	1988	1989	1990	1991
R&D as percentage of manufacturing output	4.13	4.37	4.65	4.74	5.13	5.40	5.42	5.65	5.98	6.60

Source: OECD, *National Accounts*; Österreichisches Statistisches Handbuch.

BASIC STATISTICS:

INTERNATIONAL COMPARISONS

	Units	Reference period[1]	Australia	Austria
Population				
Total	Thousands	1991	17 292	7 823
Inhabitants per sq. km	Number	1991	2	93
Net average annual increase over previous 10 years	%	1991	1.5	0.3
Employment				
Total civilian employment (TCE)[2]	Thousands	1991	7 705	3 482
Of which: Agriculture	% of TCE		5.5	7.4
Industry	% of TCE		24.2	36.9
Services	% of TCE		70.4	55.8
Gross domestic product (GDP)				
At current prices and current exchange rates	Bill. US$	1991	297.4	164.7
Per capita	US$		17 200	21 048
At current prices using current PPP's[3]	Bill. US$	1991	280	135.6
Per capita	US$		16 195	17 329
Average annual volume growth over previous 5 years	%	1991	2.8	3.3
Gross fixed capital formation (GFCF)	% of GDP	1991	20.5	25.1
Of which: Machinery and equipment	% of GDP		8.8	10.4
Residential construction	% of GDP		4.6	4.6 (90)
Average annual volume growth over previous 5 years	%	1991	0.3	5.2
Gross saving ratio[4]	% of GDP	1991	17.2	25.6
General government				
Current expenditure on goods and services	% of GDP	1991	18.3	18.2
Current disbursements[5]	% of GDP	1991	36.6	45.7
Current receipts	% of GDP	1991	33.7	47.2
Net official development assistance	% of GDP	1991	0.35	0.33
Indicators of living standards				
Private consumption per capita using current PPP's[3]	US$	1991	9 827	9 591
Passenger cars, per 1 000 inhabitants	Number	1990	430	382
Telephones, per 1 000 inhabitants	Number	1990	448 (89)	589
Television sets, per 1 000 inhabitants	Number	1989	484	475
Doctors, per 1 000 inhabitants	Number	1991	2	2.1
Infant mortality per 1 000 live births	Number	1991	7.1	7.4
Wages and prices (average annual increase over previous 5 years)				
Wages (earnings or rates according to availability)	%	1991	5.4	5.2
Consumer prices	%	1991	6.7	2.5
Foreign trade				
Exports of goods, fob*	Mill. US$	1991	39 764	40 985
As % of GDP	%		13.4	24.9
Average annual increase over previous 5 years	%		13.2	12.8
Imports of goods, cif*	Mill. US$	1991	38 844	48 914
As % of GDP	%		13.1	29.7
Average annual increase over previous 5 years	%		10.1	13.7
Total official reserves[6]	Mill. SDR's	1991	11 432	6 591
As ratio of average monthly imports of goods	Ratio		3.5	1.6

* At current prices and exchange rates.
1. Unless otherwise stated.
2. According to the definitions used in OECD *Labour Force Statistics*.
3. PPP's = Purchasing Power Parities.
4. Gross saving = Gross national disposable income minus private and government consumption.
5. Current disbursements = Current expenditure on goods and services plus current transfers and payments of property income.
6. Gold included in reserves is valued at 35 SDR's per ounce. End of year.
7. Including Luxembourg.

EMPLOYMENT OPPORTUNITIES

Economics Department, OECD

The Economics Department of the OECD offers challenging and rewarding opportunities to economists interested in applied policy analysis in an international environment. The Department's concerns extend across the entire field of economic policy analysis, both macro-economic and micro-economic. Its main task is to provide, for discussion by committees of senior officials from Member countries, documents and papers dealing with current policy concerns. Within this programme of work, three major responsibilities are:

- to prepare regular surveys of the economies of individual Member countries;
- to issue full twice-yearly reviews of the economic situation and prospects of the OECD countries in the context of world economic trends;
- to analyse specific policy issues in a medium-term context for theOECD as a whole, and to a lesser extent for the non-OECD countries.

The documents prepared for these purposes, together with much of the Department's other economic work, appear in published form in the *OECD Economic Outlook, OECD Economic Surveys, OECD Economic Studies* and the Department's *Working Papers* series.

The Department maintains a world econometric model, INTERLINK, which plays an important role in the preparation of the policy analyses and twice-yearly projections. The availability of extensive cross-country data bases and good computer resources facilitates comparative empirical analysis, much of which is incorporated into the model.

The Department is made up of about 75 professional economists from a variety of backgrounds and Member countries. Most projects are carried out by small teams and last from four to eighteen months. Within the Department, ideas and points of view are widely discussed; there is a lively professional interchange, and all professional staff have the opportunity to contribute actively to the programme of work.

Skills the Economics Department is looking for:

a) Solid competence in using the tools of both micro-economic and macro-economic theory to answer policy questions. Experience indicates that this normally requires the equivalent of a PH.D. in economics or substantial relevant professional experience to compensate for a lower degree.

b) Solid knowledge of economic statistics and quantitative methods; this includes how to identify data, estimate structural relationships, apply basic techniques of time series analysis, and test hypotheses. It is essential to be able to interpret results sensibly in an economic policy context.

c) A keen interest in and knowledge of policy issues, economic developments and their political/social contexts.

d) Interest and experience in analysing questions posed by policy-makers and presenting the results to them effectively and judiciously. Thus, work experience in government agencies or policy research institutions is an advantage.

e) The ability to write clearly, effectively, and to the point. The OECD is a bilingual organisation with French and English as the official languages. Candidates must have excellent knowledge of one of these languages, and some knowledge of the other. Knowledge of other languages might also be an advantage for certain posts.

f) For some posts, expertise in a particular area may be important, but a successful candidate is expected to be able to work on a broader range of topics relevant to the work of the Department. Thus, except in rare cases, the Department does not recruit narrow specialists.

g) The Department works on a tight time schedule and strict deadlines. Moreover, much of the work in the Department is carried out in small groups of economists. Thus, the ability to work with other economists from a variety of cultural and professional backgrounds, to supervise junior staff, and to produce work on time is important.

General Information

The salary for recruits depends on educational and professional background. Positions carry a basic salary from FF 262 512 or FF 323 916 for Administrators (economists) and from FF 375 708 for Principal Administrators (senior economists). This may be supplemented by expatriation and/or family allowances, depending on nationality, residence and family situation. Initial appointments are for a fixed term of two to three years.

Vacancies are open to candidates from OECD Member countries. The Organisation seeks to maintain an appropriate balance between female and male staff and among nationals from Member countries.

For further information on employment opportunities in the Economics Department, contact:

Administrative Unit
Economics Department
OECD
2, rue André-Pascal
75775 PARIS CEDEX 16
FRANCE

Applications citing "ECSUR", together with a detailed *curriculum vitae* in English or French, should be sent to the Head of Personnel at the above address.

MAIN SALES OUTLETS OF OECD PUBLICATIONS
PRINCIPAUX POINTS DE VENTE DES PUBLICATIONS DE L'OCDE

ARGENTINA – ARGENTINE
Carlos Hirsch S.R.L.
Galería Güemes, Florida 165, 4° Piso
1333 Buenos Aires   Tel. (1) 331.1787 y 331.2391
Telefax: (1) 331.1787

AUSTRALIA – AUSTRALIE
D.A. Information Services
648 Whitehorse Road, P.O.B 163
Mitcham, Victoria 3132   Tel. (03) 873.4411
Telefax: (03) 873.5679

AUSTRIA – AUTRICHE
Gerold & Co.
Graben 31
Wien I   Tel. (0222) 533.50.14

BELGIUM – BELGIQUE
Jean De Lannoy
Avenue du Roi 202
B-1060 Bruxelles   Tel. (02) 538.51.69/538.08.41
Telefax: (02) 538.08.41

CANADA
Renouf Publishing Company Ltd.
1294 Algoma Road
Ottawa, ON K1B 3W8   Tel. (613) 741.4333
Telefax: (613) 741.5439
Stores:
61 Sparks Street
Ottawa, ON K1P 5R1   Tel. (613) 238.8985
211 Yonge Street
Toronto, ON M5B 1M4   Tel. (416) 363.3171
Telefax: (416)363.59.63

Les Éditions La Liberté Inc.
3020 Chemin Sainte-Foy
Sainte-Foy, PQ G1X 3V6   Tel. (418) 658.3763
Telefax: (418) 658.3763

Federal Publications Inc.
165 University Avenue, Suite 701
Toronto, ON M5H 3B8   ˙ Tel. (416) 860.1611
Telefax: (416) 860.1608

Les Publications Fédérales
1185 Université
Montréal, QC H3B 3A7   Tel. (514) 954.1633
Telefax : (514) 954.1635

CHINA – CHINE
China National Publications Import
Export Corporation (CNPIEC)
16 Gongti E. Road, Chaoyang District
P.O. Box 88 or 50
Beijing 100704 PR   Tel. (01) 506.6688
Telefax: (01) 506.3101

DENMARK – DANEMARK
Munksgaard Book and Subscription Service
35, Nørre Søgade, P.O. Box 2148
DK-1016 København K   Tel. (33) 12.85.70
Telefax: (33) 12.93.87

FINLAND – FINLANDE
Akateeminen Kirjakauppa
Keskuskatu 1, P.O. Box 128
00100 Helsinki

Subscription Services/Agence d'abonnements :
P.O. Box 23
00371 Helsinki   Tel. (358 0) 12141
Telefax: (358 0) 121.4450

FRANCE
OECD/OCDE
Mail Orders/Commandes par correspondance:
2, rue André-Pascal
75775 Paris Cedex 16   Tel. (33-1) 45.24.82.00
Telefax: (33-1) 49.10.42.76
Telex: 640048 OCDE

OECD Bookshop/Librairie de l'OCDE :
33, rue Octave-Feuillet
75016 Paris   Tel. (33-1) 45.24.81.67
(33-1) 45.24.81.81
Documentation Française
29, quai Voltaire
75007 Paris   Tel. 40.15.70.00
Gibert Jeune (Droit-Économie)
6, place Saint-Michel
75006 Paris   Tel. 43.25.91.19
Librairie du Commerce International
10, avenue d'Iéna
75016 Paris   Tel. 40.73.34.60
Librairie Dunod
Université Paris-Dauphine
Place du Maréchal de Lattre de Tassigny
75016 Paris   Tel. (1) 44.05.40.13
Librairie Lavoisier
11, rue Lavoisier
75008 Paris   Tel. 42.65.39.95
Librairie L.G.D.J. - Montchrestien
20, rue Soufflot
75005 Paris   Tel. 46.33.89.85
Librairie des Sciences Politiques
30, rue Saint-Guillaume
75007 Paris   Tel. 45.48.36.02
P.U.F.
49, boulevard Saint-Michel
75005 Paris   Tel. 43.25.83.40
Librairie de l'Université
12a, rue Nazareth
13100 Aix-en-Provence   Tel. (16) 42.26.18.08
Documentation Française
165, rue Garibaldi
69003 Lyon   Tel. (16) 78.63.32.23
Librairie Decitre
29, place Bellecour
69002 Lyon   Tel. (16) 72.40.54.54

GERMANY – ALLEMAGNE
OECD Publications and Information Centre
August-Bebel-Allee 6
D-53175 Bonn 2   Tel. (0228) 959.120
Telefax: (0228) 959.12.17

GREECE – GRÈCE
Librairie Kauffmann
Mavrokordatou 9
106 78 Athens   Tel. (01) 32.55.321
Telefax: (01) 36.33.967

HONG-KONG
Swindon Book Co. Ltd.
13–15 Lock Road
Kowloon, Hong Kong   Tel. 366.80.31
Telefax: 739.49.75

HUNGARY – HONGRIE
Euro Info Service
POB 1271
1464 Budapest   Tel. (1) 111.62.16
Telefax : (1) 111.60.61

ICELAND – ISLANDE
Mál Mog Menning
Laugavegi 18, Pósthólf 392
121 Reykjavik   Tel. 162.35.23

INDIA – INDE
Oxford Book and Stationery Co.
Scindia House
New Delhi 110001   Tel.(11) 331.5896/5308
Telefax: (11) 332.5993
17 Park Street
Calcutta 700016   Tel. 240832

INDONESIA – INDONÉSIE
Pdii-Lipi
P.O. Box 269/JKSMG/88
Jakarta 12790   Tel. 583467
Telex: 62 875

IRELAND – IRLANDE
TDC Publishers – Library Suppliers
12 North Frederick Street
Dublin 1   Tel. (01) 874.48.35
Telefax: (01) 874.84.16

ISRAEL
Electronic Publications only
Publications électroniques seulement
Praedicta
5 Shatna Street
P.O. Box 34030
Jerusalem 91340   Tel. (2) 52.84.90/1/2
Telefax: (2) 52.84.93

ITALY – ITALIE
Libreria Commissionaria Sansoni
Via Duca di Calabria 1/1
50125 Firenze   Tel. (055) 64.54.15
Telefax: (055) 64.12.57
Via Bartolini 29
20155 Milano   Tel. (02) 36.50.83
Editrice e Libreria Herder
Piazza Montecitorio 120
00186 Roma   Tel. 679.46.28
Telefax: 678.47.51
Libreria Hoepli
Via Hoepli 5
20121 Milano   Tel. (02) 86.54.46
Telefax: (02) 805.28.86
Libreria Scientifica
Dott. Lucio de Biasio 'Aeiou'
Via Coronelli, 6
20146 Milano   Tel. (02) 48.95.45.52
Telefax: (02) 48.95.45.48

JAPAN – JAPON
OECD Publications and Information Centre
Landic Akasaka Building
2-3-4 Akasaka, Minato-ku
Tokyo 107   Tel. (81.3) 3586.2016
Telefax: (81.3) 3584.7929

KOREA – CORÉE
Kyobo Book Centre Co. Ltd.
P.O. Box 1658, Kwang Hwa Moon
Seoul   Tel. 730.78.91
Telefax: 735.00.30

MALAYSIA – MALAISIE
Co-operative Bookshop Ltd.
University of Malaya
P.O. Box 1127, Jalan Pantai Baru
59700 Kuala Lumpur
Malaysia   Tel. 756.5000/756.5425
Telefax: 757.3661

MEXICO – MEXIQUE
Revistas y Periodicos Internacionales S.A. de C.V.
Florencia 57 - 1004
Mexico, D.F. 06600   Tel. 207.81.00
Telefax : 208.39.79

NETHERLANDS – PAYS-BAS
SDU Uitgeverij Plantijnstraat
Externe Fondsen
Postbus 20014
2500 EA's-Gravenhage   Tel. (070) 37.89.880
Voor bestellingen: Telefax: (070) 34.75.778

NEW ZEALAND
NOUVELLE-ZÉLANDE
Legislation Services
P.O. Box 12418
Thorndon, Wellington   Tel. (04) 496.5652
                              Telefax: (04) 496.5698

NORWAY – NORVÈGE
Narvesen Info Center – NIC
Bertrand Narvesens vei 2
P.O. Box 6125 Etterstad
0602 Oslo 6   Tel. (022) 57.33.00
                              Telefax: (022) 68.19.01

PAKISTAN
Mirza Book Agency
65 Shahrah Quaid-E-Azam
Lahore 54000   Tel. (42) 353.601
                              Telefax: (42) 231.730

PHILIPPINE – PHILIPPINES
International Book Center
5th Floor, Filipinas Life Bldg.
Ayala Avenue
Metro Manila   Tel. 81.96.76
                              Telex 23312 RHP PH

PORTUGAL
Livraria Portugal
Rua do Carmo 70-74
Apart. 2681
1200 Lisboa   Tel.: (01) 347.49.82/5
                              Telefax: (01) 347.02.64

SINGAPORE – SINGAPOUR
Gower Asia Pacific Pte Ltd.
Golden Wheel Building
41, Kallang Pudding Road, No. 04-03
Singapore 1334   Tel. 741.5166
                              Telefax: 742.9356

SPAIN – ESPAGNE
Mundi-Prensa Libros S.A.
Castelló 37, Apartado 1223
Madrid 28001   Tel. (91) 431.33.99
                              Telefax: (91) 575.39.98

Libreria Internacional AEDOS
Consejo de Ciento 391
08009 – Barcelona   Tel. (93) 488.30.09
                              Telefax: (93) 487.76.59
Llibreria de la Generalitat
Palau Moja
Rambla dels Estudis, 118
08002 – Barcelona
            (Subscripcions) Tel. (93) 318.80.12
            (Publicacions) Tel. (93) 302.67.23
                              Telefax: (93) 412.18.54

SRI LANKA
Centre for Policy Research
c/o Colombo Agencies Ltd.
No. 300-304, Galle Road
Colombo 3   Tel. (1) 574240, 573551-2
                              Telefax: (1) 575394, 510711

SWEDEN – SUÈDE
Fritzes Information Center
Box 16356
Regeringsgatan 12
106 47 Stockholm   Tel. (08) 690.90.90
                              Telefax: (08) 20.50.21

Subscription Agency/Agence d'abonnements :
Wennergren-Williams Info AB
P.O. Box 1305
171 25 Solna   Tel. (08) 705.97.50
                              Téléfax : (08) 27.00.71

SWITZERLAND – SUISSE
Maditec S.A. (Books and Periodicals - Livres
et périodiques)
Chemin des Palettes 4
Case postale 266
1020 Renens   Tel. (021) 635.08.65
                              Telefax: (021) 635.07.80

Librairie Payot S.A.
4, place Pépinet
CP 3212
1002 Lausanne   Tel. (021) 341.33.48
                              Telefax: (021) 341.33.45

Librairie Unilivres
6, rue de Candolle
1205 Genève   Tel. (022) 320.26.23
                              Telefax: (022) 329.73.18

Subscription Agency/Agence d'abonnements :
Dynapresse Marketing S.A.
38 avenue Vibert
1227 Carouge   Tel.: (022) 308.07.89
                              Telefax : (022) 308.07.99

See also – Voir aussi :
OECD Publications and Information Centre
August-Bebel-Allee 6
D-53175 Bonn 2 (Germany)   Tel. (0228) 959.120
                              Telefax: (0228) 959.12.17

TAIWAN – FORMOSE
Good Faith Worldwide Int'l. Co. Ltd.
9th Floor, No. 118, Sec. 2
Chung Hsiao E. Road
Taipei   Tel. (02) 391.7396/391.7397
                              Telefax: (02) 394.9176

THAILAND – THAÏLANDE
Suksit Siam Co. Ltd.
113, 115 Fuang Nakhon Rd.
Opp. Wat Rajbopith
Bangkok 10200   Tel. (662) 225.9531/2
                              Telefax: (662) 222.5188

TURKEY – TURQUIE
Kültür Yayinlari Is-Türk Ltd. Sti.
Atatürk Bulvari No. 191/Kat 13
Kavaklidere/Ankara   Tel. 428.11.40 Ext. 2458
Dolmabahce Cad. No. 29
Besiktas/Istanbul   Tel. 260.71.88
                              Telex: 43482B

UNITED KINGDOM – ROYAUME-UNI
HMSO
Gen. enquiries   Tel. (071) 873 0011
Postal orders only:
P.O. Box 276, London SW8 5DT
Personal Callers HMSO Bookshop
49 High Holborn, London WC1V 6HB
                              Telefax: (071) 873 8200
Branches at: Belfast, Birmingham, Bristol, Edin-
burgh, Manchester

UNITED STATES – ÉTATS-UNIS
OECD Publications and Information Centre
2001 L Street N.W., Suite 700
Washington, D.C. 20036-4910 Tel. (202) 785.6323
                              Telefax: (202) 785.0350

VENEZUELA
Libreria del Este
Avda F. Miranda 52, Aptdo. 60337
Edificio Galipán
Caracas 106   Tel. 951.1705/951.2307/951.1297
                              Telegram: Libreste Caracas

Subscription to OECD periodicals may also be
placed through main subscription agencies.

Les abonnements aux publications périodiques de
l'OCDE peuvent être souscrits auprès des
principales agences d'abonnement.

Orders and inquiries from countries where Distribu-
tors have not yet been appointed should be sent to:
OECD Publications Service, 2 rue André-Pascal,
75775 Paris Cedex 16, France.

Les commandes provenant de pays où l'OCDE n'a
pas encore désigné de distributeur devraient être
adressées à : OCDE, Service des Publications,
2, rue André-Pascal, 75775 Paris Cedex 16, France.

3-1994

PRINTED IN FRANCE

•

OECD PUBLICATIONS
2 rue André-Pascal
75775 PARIS CEDEX 16
No. 47197
(10 94 11 1) ISBN 92-64-14128-6
ISSN 0376-6438

•